GOING TO LIVE ON THE

FRENCH RIVIERA

CHARLES DAVEY

howto**books**

Published by How To Books Ltd,
Spring Hill House, Spring Hill Road
Begbroke, Oxford OX5 1RX
Tel: (01865) 375794 Fax: (01865) 379162
email: info@howtobooks.co.uk
http://www.howtobooks.co.uk

First edition 2006

British Library Cataloguing in Publication Data
A catalogue record for this book is available from
the British Library.

ISBN 13: 978 1 84528 118 2
ISBN 10: 1 84528 118 7

Produced for How To Books by Deer Park Productions, Tavistock
Typeset by *specialist* publishing services ltd, Montgomery
Cover design by Baseline Arts Ltd, Oxford
Printed and bound by Bell & Bain Ltd, Glasgow

Note: The material contained in this book is set out in good
faith for general guidance and no liability can be accepted
for loss or expense incurred as a result of relying in particular
circumstances on statements made in the book. The laws and
regulations are complex and liable to change, and readers should
check the current position with the relevant authorities before
making personal arrangements.

Contents

Take more of your money with you

If you're planning a move to the French Riviera it's likely that the last thing on your mind is foreign exchange. However, at some point you will have to change your hard earned money into euros. Unfortunately, exchange rates are constantly moving and as a result can have a big impact on the amount of money you have to create your dream home.

For example, if you look at the euro during 2005 you can see how this movement can affect your capital. Sterling against the euro was as high as 1.5124 and as low as 1.4086. This meant that if you had £200,000 you could have ended up with as much as €302,480 or as little as €281,720, a difference of over €20,000.

It is possible to avoid this pitfall by fixing a rate through a **forward contract**. A small deposit will secure you a rate for anywhere up to 2 years in advance and by doing so provides the security of having the currency you need at a guaranteed cost.

Another option if you have time on your side is a **limit order**. This is used when you want to achieve a rate that is currently not available. You set the rate that you want and the market is then monitored. As soon as that rate is achieved the currency is purchased for you.

If you need to act swiftly and your capital is readily available then it is most likely that you will use a **spot transaction**. This is the *Buy now, Pay now* option where you get the most competitive rate on the day.

To ensure you get the most for you money it's a good idea to use a foreign exchange specialist such as Currencies Direct. As an alternative to your bank, Currencies Direct is able to offer you extremely competitive exchange rates, no commission charges and free transfers*. This can mean considerable savings on your transfer when compared to using a bank.

*Over £5,000

Information provided by Currencies Direct.
www.currenciesdirect.com   Tel: 0845 389 1729
Email: info@currenciesdirect.com

Preface

Whilst there are many sources of information in English about the French Riviera there has to date been no one comprehensive guide for those moving to the area. I hope that you will find that this book fills that gap. My wife and I, our three children and pets, have spent six years living on the French Riviera and much of the information contained in this book is based on personal knowledge and experience, including in relation to schools and medical services. Whilst inevitably some of the content is of general application for people moving anywhere in France, I have endeavoured to ensure that most of it relates specifically to your move to the Riviera.

I hope that you will enjoy your time in this beautiful region of France, and that you will find this book informative, practical and interesting. Good luck!

Please note that although I have used 'he', throughout the book this is purely a question of style, and is intended to embrace male and female.

Whilst every effort has been made to ensure that the information in this book is accurate, readers should appreciate that it is for general guidance only. No legal responsibility will be accepted by the author or publishers for the accuracy of the information and guidance or for any loss or expense incurred from relying on it. Readers should always ensure that they obtain up to date and specific advice from an appropriate expert or government department before entering into any commitment.

Charles Davey

France and Provence-Alpes-Côte d'Azur (PACA)

1
Welcome to
the French Riviera

The area known as Provence is situated between the Rhône to the west and the Italian border to the east, and stretches from the Alps in the north to the Mediterranean coastline in the south. The Côte d'Azur covers only the departments of the Alpes-Maritimes and the Var in the south east corner of Provence. The term French Riviera is a term introduced by the Victorians. The French Riviera starts at the Italian border, though there is disagreement as to how far it extends westwards beyond the Alpes-Maritimes into the Var. Some would say that it ends at the boundary between the two departments, whilst I have heard estate agents apply it to the coastline as far as St. Tropez.

Certainly the Côte d'Azur, and especially the Alpes-Maritimes, is by far the most popular part of Provence with tourists and foreign property buyers alike. Both are drawn by the micro-climate that makes it the sunniest part of France, blessed with long hot summers and extremely mild winters. The French themselves are also drawn to the PACA area (Provence-Alpes-Côte d'Azur), which is the third most popular region for French citizens to move to.

Whilst the regional PACA capital, Marseille, has a population of about 1 million and is the second city of France, it is easily surpassed by Nice as a centre for tourism. Nice is the capital of the Côte d'Azur and has a modest population of 350,000, yet its airport is the second busiest airport in France.

The Côte d'Azur remains as popular as ever, despite the competition from Eastern Europe and other cheaper destinations. Last year 9,750,000 passengers went through Nice airport, an increase of 4.4% on the previous year – an additional 350,000 passengers. Whilst this rise was partly a result of greater volume of traffic from French airports, the percentage rise in international travellers using the airport was greater. A relatively new development is the large number of Russian visitors, currently estimated at 100,000 a year.

New destinations from Nice airport include Marrakech (Atlas Blue), Budapest (Sky Europe) and also Crete, putting the Côte d'Azur within easy access of the inhabitants of these locations.

The Alpes-Maritimes has for decades been the most popular French destination for British holiday-makers, both for those seeking to buy a property and for those who determine to live in France. The Victorians played a particularly important part in the development of the coastal areas, such as the building of the majestic hotels along Le Promenade des Anglais in Nice. Today English speakers arriving here will find a wide range of businesses and services run by and/or for English speaking communities.

'Purgatory or Paradise?' was the heading of the *Riviera Times* in its November 2005 issue. Mediterranean Editions, the owners of the paper and of sister Italian and German editions, had carried out a survey of 1,000 readers from these three large foreign populations living on the Côte d'Azur. Three issues seemed to be dominant among the concerns of all three nationalities: security, cost of living and road safety (though the latter was much less of a concern to Italian readers). Whilst a significant proportion of *Riviera Times* respondents reported having been the victim of crime, 50% felt safe living in the area. A staggering 85% of readers of the *Riviera Times* thought that the locals' driving was risky (55%) or life threatening (30%), and almost two thirds of them found living in the region 'expensive' or 'very expensive'.

THE CÔTE D'AZUR: THE PLACE AND THE PEOPLE

Climate

The climate on the French Riviera is hot – and set to become even hotter, with estimated temperature rises being greater here than in many other parts of Europe. OMERC, the national body responsible for monitoring climate change, has recently reported that average temperatures across the Côte d'Azur have risen by 4–5 degrees in summer and 2–3 degrees in the winter. It is claimed that by 2100 the region's climate will be akin to that of Tunisia.

The people

There have been claims that the local population is lazy and dishonest. This is said to account for the high number of sick notes issued each year (well above the average for the rest of France), or the fact that 150,000 residents on the coast have failed to purchase a television licence. Corruption has been a recurrent problem in the region. In 1999 the newly arrived prosecutor for Nice, Eric de

3

Montgolfier, commented that Nice did not really behave as if it was a part of France. More recently he explained that Nice was characterised by a system of patronage (soft speak for nepotism and corruption) dating back a long time and that one could not simply put an immediate end to it!

The people of the Côte d'Azur have a reputation amongst the French for being rather cold and unfriendly. It is said that when they greet you they hold out their arms, but never close them around you. It is unwise, however, to come with any preconceived ideas, and better to avoid making any such generalisations. You should also remember that a large proportion of the people living on the Côte d'Azur do not originate here at all – the area has grown rapidly over the last few decades with large numbers moving in from other parts of France, and thousands of economic immigrants especially from Portugal and Italy. You may find that any unfriendliness you do come across is not from a local at all!

Racism is definitely a problem in the region, particularly against Arabs and black immigrants. SOS Racisme has had numerous complaints from young people from ethnic minority groups who complain that they are being refused entrance to bars and clubs along the coast of the Alpes-Maritimes and the Var. SOS Racisme carried out its own survey during 2005 and estimated that around 40% of the clubs and bars they visited operated a race policy. Recently a right wing charity that offered food to the destitute was providing only a pork-based soup, thereby effectively preventing those in the local Arab population from benefiting.

Italians are undoubtedly the largest foreign contingent on the coast, with many local businesses owned by Italians or those of Italian descent. In fact their numbers are falling, with far more selling property on the French Riviera than buying. One reason is said to be the amnesty offered by the Italian authorities permitting Italians to repatriate money illegally transferred out of Italy.

It was only two years ago that parts of the local English press were referring to the area as the 'Crotte d'Azur' owing to the vast quantity of dog excrement left by dogs (or should I say their owners) on the streets. Town Councils along the coast have introduced measures to counter this, including free bags. La Ville de Cannes has special motorbikes with hoovers that patrol the streets. They have proved very effective, though expensive.

The region

The Alpes-Maritimes is situated in an earthquake zone and saw a substantial loss of life and considerable destruction in the last earthquake in 1887. The region is also subject to many frequent earth tremors. New building regulations were introduced in 1994, primarily covering apartment blocks, though the extent of compliance with these is questionable. The likelihood of a further earthquake in the Alpes-Maritimes at some point during the next 200 years does not appear to restrict the rise in property prices in the department, nor indeed in Monaco where prices are substantially higher. The neighbouring Var has been subjected to 'natural' disasters in more recent years – the summer of 2003 saw over 20,000 hectares of woodland destroyed by fires. Seven people lost their lives, and 70 firefighters were injured.

Despite these natural hazards, the popularity of the Côte d'Azur is such that many property owners are able to let out their properties during much of the summer, from as early as May to as late as mid-October, earning far more than they could on a long-term rental.

Indeed, some owner-occupiers let out their own homes for a month or even longer in the summer, and take their holidays elsewhere, move in with friends or find cheap short-term accommodation.

Crime

All tourist regions attract crime, and the Côte d'Azur is certainly no exception. Always keep your car doors locked, especially in slow-moving traffic. All too often motorists fall prey to a couple of youths who draw up on a moped alongside a stationary car. One quickly dismounts, opens a car door and searches for valuables, often threatening the occupants of the car with a knife. Within seconds the thief is again on the back of the revving moped and speeds away, weaving between the gridlocked vehicles, leaving the unhappy motorist unable to pursue. In recent months the Alpes-Maritime Prefecture has announced a plan of action to counter this menace, known as *vol à la portière*. Leaflets have been given out at airports and warnings posted. More recently the authorities have installed CCTV security cameras at some of the most vulnerable locations such as the A8 exits at Nice Est and Nice Ouest. The ALHU (Aide Linguistique Humanitaire et d'Urgence) is now generally available to translate between non-French speaking victims and the police. If you need their assistance you can contact them 24 hours a day on 04 75 68 87 97 or 06 71 91 77 43.

Of course, thanks to more sophisticated security and alarm systems cars are becoming more difficult to break into and steal. However, undeterred, the more imaginative of the region's criminal fraternity are abusing the law in France that requires drivers to stop to give assistance to those in difficulty. Many people here have fallen victim to the thief who has pretended to be injured and then hopped into their vehicle and driven it away. Others are persuaded to get out to examine a supposedly faulty exhaust, only to find themselves left standing in the road as the culprit speeds away in their car.

Crime is at its highest during July and August, with gangs, in some cases of young children, travelling to the area from across the border in Italy and further afield. Some offenders are well-dressed and employ a range of aids and strategies, such as using forceps to remove items from pockets, or 'accidentally' squirting ketchup on someone's jacket, helping them remove the jacket, and clandestinely extracting the person's wallet in the process. Tourists and residents need to be distrustful and discrete. Avoid handling large amounts of cash in public view.

In 2005 the *préfet* of les Alpes-Maritimes complained that the department was the worst place for crime in France outside Paris.

Mafia groups are known to be active in the region, often based in Eastern Europe. Their victims, other than tourists, are often the beggars to be found at many locations in the south west, who are forced to hand over their takings. Many are Romanian, Bosnian or Polish. The same is true of many of the prostitutes on the streets of Nice, brought here against their will.

PRACTICAL HELP

British consular offices: the consular office in Nice is no longer in use. The part-time Honorary Consul in Nice is still contactable, though it is advisable to contact the Consulate in Marseille initially (04 91 15 72 10).

Adapt in France (Centre de Vie, Place Mejane, 06560 Sophia Antipolis, contact Sylvie Kermin Coiffier on 04 93 65 33 79). This association, founded only a few years ago by a lady from Brittany who was conscious of the lack of information and resources for foreigners in the region, now holds numerous workshops in English. Recent topics have included buying and renting accommodation, insurance, mortgage finance, setting up a business, social and welfare rights, healthcare, banking services, motoring, education, childcare, taxes, French inheritance rules and taxation, public transport, animal issues, French business culture and utilities.

Accueil des Ville Françaises (AVF) is a nationwide organisation set up in 1964 to help people newly arrived in a town or region. There are a number of centres on the Côte d'Azur. The association provides pre-arrival support in the form of local information, a guide of the town, practical assistance relating to a wide range of issues including schooling, medical services, and issues to do with utilities and the local council. Once you have arrived the AVF provides you with the opportunity of meeting both other newcomers and those who are already well-established. On the Riviera this will mean people from a wide range of nationalities, including many French people. The AVF arranges classes for diverse social and cultural activities including French classes and computer lessons, as well as social events and outings. The classes are all run by volunteers, are inexpensive and an excellent means of meeting people. The majority of the volunteers who staff the AVF branches are French, and the help they provide is mostly in French. However many foreigners, especially those who can speak English, are joining the AVF as volunteers to welcome new arrivals. AVF has branches in Antibes, Cannes (04 93 94 41 82), Cannes La Bocca, Grasse (04 93 36 98 30), Mandelieu (04 92 97 94 76), Nice (04 93 34 89 08) and Sophia Antipolis (04 93 65 43 00).

A very useful source of information, relatively recently established, is the website AMB Côte d'Azur (www.amb-cotedazur.com). It is run by a husband and wife team Alice and Nigel Barker. AMB Côte d'Azur is again a non-profit making association. The website features regular articles on aspects of living in France, and in particular on the French Riviera. It includes information on local towns, events and festivals, interviews with local writers and an extensive list of links to other useful sites.

There are a number of other sources of information and assistance to English speakers detailed later in this book, including the very well-established *Riviera Reporter,* and the website www.angloinfo.com.

PARTICULAR LOCATIONS

Nice

Nice is a busy city, with the usual advantages and disadvantages of other cities, including areas with extremely poor housing, crime and violence. There are, of course, pleasant residential areas, in particular in the hills with views overlooking Nice and the coast. There has been substantial building of new properties in the nearby town of St. Laurent-du-Var. This area has been popular with many owing to lower property prices than in most other locations along the coast, the proximity of the airport, the Cap 3000 shopping complex, the motorway and the International School of Nice.

Nice is currently a congestion nightmare. Large parts of the city have been in chaos for some time owing to the construction of its tramway. The work has had a dramatic impact on businesses on the Avenue de la République, with business owners' losses only partly being offset by the compensation available. The first of the three lines is not now due to open until late in 2007 after the discovery of an archaeological site, and of asbestos in some drainage channels, caused major disruption to the progress of the scheme. It is hoped and expected that the tramway – due to be completed some time after 2015 – will eventually ease congestion in the city, and thus allow Nice to cater for more visitors.

Cannoε

Cannes is always busy, with many conferences and exhibitions being held here in addition to the internationally famous Cannes Film festival (Festival de Cannes) which takes place in May each year. Cannes is accessible from Nice and Marseille via the A8 motorway, and connected to both cities by rail. There is also a sea link from Cannes to both Nice and Monaco, and a helicopter link from Cannes-Mandelieu airport to Nice airport. In addition to extensive night life, Cannes has three cinemas.

L'Institut de Stanislas is generally recognised as one of the best schools outside of Paris. Educating children from *petite section* to post-bac it has a 100% pass rate for the *baccalauréat*.

One of the most sought-after areas in Cannes is La Californie.

Substantial construction is taking place of residential accommodation at more affordable prices at *La Croix des Gardes*.

Antibes

There are numerous British and other English speakers based in Antibes, many working in the yachting industry. The presence of

English speakers is, some would say, a little too obvious in the centre of Antibes, and feelings amongst the locals are mixed. The town centre has benefited commercially from the presence of a number of British businesses, including the Antibes bookshop, the food store Geoffrey's of London, several offices, shops serving the yachting industry, and a number of pubs.

Mandelieu-La-Napoule

Situated between Cannes and the departmental border with the Var, and between the Massif de l'Esterel and the wooded hills of Tanneron, Mandelieu-La-Napoule has a total of six ports and has more moorings for pleasure boats than any other resort in the Alpes-Maritimes. It is ideal for practising water sports – you can even watch the Oxford and Cambridge boat crews race against each other along a section of the river Siagne. Each February the town celebrates the *Festival de la Mimosa*.

Mandelieu-La-Napoule is also known for its quality golf courses.

The Château de la Napoule is home to the complete works of the American artist Henry Clews who was responsible for renovating the chateau.

Mougins

Mougins is an interesting and well-preserved medieval hilltop village with an excellent selection of restaurants. The commune of Mougins is in fact one of the largest in France in terms of geographical area. Situated just to the north of Cannes it has a population of only 17,500, but boasts well over a thousand high-tech businesses at the Sophia Antipolis business park. Mougins has

11

a substantial population of English residents, as well as significant numbers of Germans, Dutch and Swedes and, of course, the international Mougins School. The Centre International School of Valbonne and the International School of Sophia Antipolis are both nearby (see Chapter 8 Schools).

The town is well equipped in terms of sports, leisure and cultural facilities. The municipal sports centre is excellent – clean, tidy and well maintained with several tennis courts. There is a good public swimming pool (Les Campelières) on the border with Le Cannet that is open air in the summer, though often crowded.

There is a cinema at nearby Mouans-Sartoux with films in French and English and with good parking facilities.

Mougins is five minutes from exit 42 on the A8 motorway. You definitely need a car: the bus service is poor, and though a train line has recently opened between Cannes and Grasse the nearest stop is probably that at Mouans-Sartoux, some 4 km from Mougins.

Property prices vary considerably depending on where you live in the commune. A new luxury three-bedroom apartment in a prestigious development within easy access of a golf course, for example, is likely to cost in the region of €500,000. A more modest two-bedroom apartment will cost around €300,000.

Villefranche-sur-mer

This small attractive seaside resort and fishing village is only 5 km from Nice. It has a pleasant sheltered sandy beach, medieval streets housing a selection of traditional restaurants and excellent views from the harbour jetty. The Citadelle, a fortress built on the water's edge, has been restored and is now used to hold cultural events.

Communications are good both by road and rail, with direct lines west to Antibes, Cannes and all the way to Marseille, and east through Nice and onwards to the Italian border.

The Saturday morning market on the Promenade de l'Octroi is well worth visiting.

Monaco

The Principality of Monaco has some 32,000 residents living in an area of only two square kilometres. Around 6,000 are *Monegasque,* with Italians and French forming the largest other national groups. Around 32,000 people travel into Monaco to work. Strictly speaking only cars with a number plate issued in Monaco or Les Alpes-Maritimes are allowed into the Principality. Drivers of other vehicles are supposed to leave them at the *Parking du chemin de pêcheurs.*

Monaco is watched over by multiple security cameras, and large numbers of policemen.

The Principality has been successful in increasing its territory by 20% by recovering land from the sea. The Grimaldi Forum is firmly established as one of the world's best conference centres.

2
Finding somewhere to live

If your stay in the area is going to be short, or your long term plans are not yet certain, then renting is obviously a sensible option. Whilst property prices on the Côte d'Azur have risen constantly for a considerable number of years now, the high cost of buying and selling property in France means that you are only likely to sell for a net profit if you keep the property for several years. Renting provides a convenient and flexible short-term option, giving you the time to learn about the area, and to mull over where would be most suitable for you to live. A major disadvantage of renting is the shortage of supply of rental properties on the Côte d'Azur, especially during the summer.

FINDING A PROPERTY TO RENT

The internet is playing an increasingly important role in the rental property market allowing you to give initial consideration to properties from the comfort of your own home, enabling you to narrow down a list of properties for viewing and reducing the number of completely wasted inspections. The most useful sites are probably www.seloger.com and www.explorimmo.com, the latter having advertisements from the main national and regional newspapers (including *Le Figaro* and *Le Monde*) available from

06.00 each day, even before the papers are available to purchase. Others sites include www.pap.fr, www.foncia.com, www.fnaim.fr, www.century21.fr and www.hestia.fr.

Two other popular sources are *Nice Matin* and the free newspapers circulated in each department and known by their department number, the 06 (*le zéro six*) for example in the Alpes-Maritimes. The English-language media also have rental advertisements, including www.angloinfo.com, the *Riviera Reporter* (www.riviera-reporter.com), *Radio Riviera* (www.riviera radio.mc) and the *Riviera Times*. There are many other websites in which British people who have purchased a holiday or retirement home in France advertise their properties for rental. In addition people often put up notices in the English bookshops, or on noticeboards in the English-speaking churches. Some doctors allow notices in their waiting rooms.

Note that some agencies place appealing newspaper advertisements for properties that do not exist in the hope that readers will telephone them. When you do telephone they will generally refuse to send you any details by post, or to discuss matters over the telephone. They will only proceed if you visit their offices where they will charge a fee of around €150–200 to register. You may be lucky and find that they do have a property on their books that does suit you, but frequently they will not, and may never have. The advantage for the prospective tenant, should such an agency have a property that fits your requirements, is that you do not have to pay the usual commission of one month's rent.

A substantial number of estate agents (*agents immobiliers*) also handle rental properties. A list of agents is available at the local *bureau de tourisme* or can be found in *Les Pages Jaunes*. Estate agents charge two months' rental (plus TVA) which is split equally between landlord and tenant. Those searching for an apartment might do well to contact a number of the *administrateurs de biens* listed in the Yellow Pages. They are agents responsible for managing blocks of flats and they often act for flat owners renting out their apartments.

Visiting a property

Even when you are only renting a property, it pays to visit more than once before committing yourself to taking it. Ideally visit the property at different times of the day, and introduce yourself to your potential neighbours. A noisy and/or unpleasant neighbour could cause serious detriment to your peaceful enjoyment of the property, and one short encounter before you sign up may be enough to enable you to avoid this. If peace and quiet during the day are important to you, watch out for those white and red signs saying '*chantier interdit*'. These notifications of building works are put up several weeks before construction work is due to start.

Remember that in France an unfurnished rental usually comes without carpets and curtains, and even kitchen and sink units or light fittings. **Always check what is included, and ensure that this is recorded in the rental agreement or a schedule attached.**

Landlords' requirements

You will need to provide the landlord or his agent with your most recent salary slips. Landlords will generally only let a property to those with proof of income at least three times the level of the rent, though they may be prepared to be flexible. You will also have to pay a deposit (*caution*) and will frequently be required to provide a guarantee (see below).

Your rights as a tenant of rented property

You will have much greater protection than you would in the UK, whether or not the agreement is in writing. These rights exist even where the agreement is in English, between English speaking landlords and tenants, and signed in the UK. As a result of relatively recent legislation tenants of furnished as well as unfurnished properties are protected, with only seasonal lettings (*les locations saisonnières*) or tenancies of secondary residences (*les résidences secondaires*) remaining outside the scope of the legislation.

Le contrat de bail or tenancy agreement

These are generally not easy documents to plough through, even for a French person. Remember the contract records the liabilities that you will have as a tenant, and if you are at all uncertain about its terms you ought to have the document fully explained to you by someone with a high level of French and ideally by a *notaire* or *avocat* who speaks English well.

Whilst a rental contract is no less valid because it is by word of mouth it is advisable to have a written contract. If you are not provided with a written contract ask for one – you have a legal right to this. The advantage of a written contract is that it proves your right to be in the property and provides certainty of the terms that were agreed, including the start date, the length of the tenancy, the level of rent and the amount of the deposit. It also gives you a written record of the landlord's name and address. A tenancy in the name of one spouse only is deemed by French law to be for the benefit of both spouses, even if the marriage is after the date of the rental agreeement. A spouse is protected, but is also subject to the obligations of the tenancy.

Note that you should not accept a sub-tenancy from a tenant of a property unless you have the written consent of the owner of the property. It is always better, however, to have a direct tenancy agreement with the proprietor.

The deposit and guarantee

A deposit of two months' rent is payable before you move into the property, in addition to the first month's rent. On top of the other expenses of moving in, this can cause cash-flow problems for many tenants. Some landlords will agree to accept half the deposit on signature of the rental agreement and wait a month or two for the balance. Other landlords require a bank guarantee for future rent payments. Tenants who are under 30 and in employment, or seeking employment, or are in receipt of a state grant or *bourse* are eligible to benefit from the *LocaPass*. Under this scheme the local body responsible for its administration pays the full value of the deposit to the landlord, with the tenant repaying it by monthly instalments. The *LocaPass* also gives the landlord a rental guarantee of up to 18 months over the first three years' rental. You should contact the UESL (L'Union d'Economie Sociale pour le Logement) on 01 44 85 81 00 to find out which body administers the scheme in your locality. You can also find out information on UESL's website www.uesl.fr or by contacting the tenants' rights organisations listed on page 26 (see also the front pages of *Les Pages Jaunes*). A landlord is not entitled to insist on rent being paid quarterly, but if you do pay rent every three months, the landlord is not entitled to a deposit.

The deposit (without any interest) should be repaid to you by the landlord at the end of the tenancy, less the cost of putting right any damage caused to the property and any unpaid rent. The landlord must make the repayment within two months of the end of the tenancy. If repayment is delayed, the tenant is entitled to interest on the amount wrongly retained. Should your landlord not repay the deposit, you should send a *lettre recommandée avec avis de reception* to him. You will be notified by La Poste whether or not the letter was received. If the landlord has not paid within eight days of receiving your letter, you have the right to take him to court to recover it. It is advisable to take advice from a tenant's rights organisation (see below) or an *avocat* before embarking on that step.

The level of rent

In practice landlords on the Côte d'Azur are free to ask whatever rent they wish. However, if a landlord wishes to increase the rent for an existing rental, the law requires him to justify the proposals for a rent review by comparison with the rentals of other properties in the area. The landlord must send a recorded delivery letter to you six months before the end of your tenancy suggesting the revised rent and providing you with details of three other similar properties in the vicinity. If you do not agree with the landlord's proposal then he must submit an application to the local *Commission de Reconciliation* with a view to reach a negotiated agreement with you with the assistance of the commission. If you cannot reach an agreement the landlord has to apply to the *Tribunal d'Instance.*

The tenant's rights to stay in the premises

French law provides that, subject to several exceptions, unfurnished tenancies let for the purposes of a primary residence must be for a minimum of three years if the landlord is a private individual (*un particulier*) or an SCI (*Société Civile Immobilière*). An SCI is a company formed especially to own and manage rental properties. If the landlord is a *personne morale*, i.e. a bank or insurance company, then a minimum period of six years applies.

A landlord is not entitled to possession of your home before the end of the agreement save in very limited circumstances such as: failure to pay rent, damage to the property, subletting without consent, or unacceptable disturbance to neighbours. Even then, the law provides that the landlord must apply to the court for an order. This can prove a lengthy process. The courts will not be quick to order an eviction of a tenant who demonstrates a willingness to put matters right, and in the case of rent arrears will generally give the tenant time to pay. Even when the landlord has obtained an order for possession it is illegal to proceed with the eviction of a tenant between the 1st November and the 15th March.

Whatever the length of the tenancy, you have the right to end it at any time by giving the requisite notice. You also have an automatic right to extend the tenancy for a further three years (or six years if the landlord is a bank or insurance company). A landlord has only limited grounds on which he can object to the renewal. To object he must demonstrate that he wishes to live in the property himself, or that the tenant has seriously breached the tenancy agreement or that he wishes to sell the property. Should you remain in the property without anything being decided then the renewal for a further three or six years is automatic.

Tenants of banks and insurance companies that are selling more than ten flats in a block benefit from enhanced protection. To obtain possession of an apartment rented by tenants with an annual income of less than 66,000 euros the landlord is obliged to find suggestions for alternative accommodation.

Minimum one-year tenancies

If a landlord can demonstrate a specific family or work reason for requiring early repossession of a property, such as a temporary posting abroad and an intention to live in the property on his return, or because of a planned marriage, he can let his property for a shorter period. He must indicate at the outset why he will need the property back and must grant the tenant a tenancy of at least twelve months. To ensure they obtain possession then, at least two months before the end of the tenancy, landlords must write to tenants stating that they still require the property for the reason stated. Failure to do this results in the law imposing a standard three-year tenancy.

Maintaining and improving the property

Tenants must keep a property in a good state of repair by carrying out such minor repairs and basic maintenance as: repairing broken windows, painting woodwork, bleeding radiators and replacing bulbs and fuses. The landlord is responsible for substantial works of maintenance and repair.

Should tenants wish to carry out any substantial work such as that involving making holes in walls they should obtain the landlord's prior written consent. A landlord, however, does not ordinarily need the tenant's consent to carry out works of maintenance and improvement to the property. A tenant is at risk of a landlord starting substantial building works that cause severe disturbance. If this happens towards the end of the tenancy the tenant may not even obtain any benefit! You should consider insisting that the landlord agrees to a note being written on the tenancy agreement that he (or his successor, if he sells) will not carry out any works of improvement without the tenant's consent.

Note that if you are unhappy with charges the landlord seeks to levy for expenditure incurred in relation to basic maintenance of the property, or the costs of heating and lighting, you are entitled to request proof of the expenditure, but you only have one month from receiving the account to challenge it.

A tenant's other rights

A landlord is not permitted to forbid the tenant from keeping a pet (landlord bans on pit bull terriers and other dangerous pets have been upheld). A landlord may not insist on the tenant paying by direct debit or direct from a tenant's salary, nor require the tenant to insure the property with a particular insurance company. A tenant has the right to work from the premises if it is his principal home, though a tenant may not receive clients or merchandise at the property. The rules are less stringent for childminders. You should note, however, that in many cases tenants of flats will be restricted in terms of working from home as they will be limited by the same rules and regulations that govern all the occupiers of residential developments that do often restrict the right to use the premises for work purposes.

Before you move into a property

Most rental agreements will require you to have an insurance policy in place prior to being handed the keys. Even if there is no such requirement, it is advisable to have immediate cover in place. A landlord may legitimately require proof of your insurance.

It is extremely important that you have a record of the condition of the property before you move in. It is standard to have an *État des Lieux* drawn up. This is a written record of the condition of the property at the time that the tenancy starts. If this is not done the property is assumed by the law to have been in a good condition at the beginning of a tenancy, unless the tenant can prove otherwise. As a tenant is legally obliged to return the property to the landlord in the condition at the commencement of the tenancy (apart from normal wear and tear), it is vital that the *État des Lieux* records any defects. A failure to do this will expose you to the risk that you will have to pay to rectify defects that were already present in the property.

An *État des Lieux* is frequently carried out by a qualified lawyer called a *huissier*, who will inspect the property before the tenant moves in and will charge between €235 and €300, the cost to be paid equally by the landlord and the tenant. I recommend that you inspect the property yourself prior to the visit and prepare a list of defects to draw to the attention of the *huissier*. You can avoid this cost by agreeing with the landlord to prepare the *État des Lieux* together. Whichever course you adopt the *État des Lieux* should be completed in duplicate, and each signed by the landlord and the tenant.

Should the landlord ask you to sign an inventory of contents ensure that you verify that it is correct. If you notice inaccuracies, in the inventory or the checklist, or in the condition of the property at a later stage, send a recorded delivery letter to the landlord or agent. I also strongly recommend taking a video of the property before or as soon as you move in, paying particular attention to any defects especially those not recorded or inadequately recorded on the *État des Lieux*. You could post the video to yourself by recorded delivery to prove the date the video was taken (ensure that the package is kept unopened). If and when you need it take it to your *avocat*, or some other person who can confirm the date that it was opened, and that the package had not previously been opened.

A second *État des Lieux* must be completed when you vacate the property and a comparison is then made with the first. I would recommend that you again keep video evidence of the condition of the property – include a recording of a news item on the television (or radio) so that you can prove that the recording was not earlier than your departure date.

Giving notice to leave

As indicated above you may give notice to leave (*le congé*) at any time. Three months' notice is generally required. To be effective the notice must be posted to the landlord by *lettre recommandée avec avis de réception* or served on the landord by a *huissier*. The three months' notice period begins on the day that the landlord receives your letter of notice. You will know when this was when you receive the notification sent to you by La Poste, stating the date of delivery.

Tenants only have to give one month's notice if they change their job, lose their job or obtain fresh employment after losing a job. This reduction in the notice period also applies where the tenant is more than sixty years old and needs to move for health reasons, or if the tenant's income falls below a certain level. When the tenant sends the notice letter they must include documentary evidence to demonstrate their entitlement to give only one month's notice. If you do not do this you will be obliged to give the full three months' notice.

Furnished tenancies

Tenants renting furnished premises as their principal residence also benefit from significant protection under French law. The contract must be for at least 12 months, and if the landlord is intending to regain possession at the end of the year, he is obliged to serve notice on the tenant at least three months before the expiry of the tenancy. If the landlord fails to do this then the tenancy is renewed automatically for a further twelve months. Even where landlords serve the correct notice in time they are not guaranteed obtaining possession. Should the tenant wish to leave he can give notice at any time and is only required to give one month's notice.

Disagreements between landlord and tenant

If you are in dispute with your landlord, the first step is to check whether you have legal expenses insurance as part of your household insurance policy. If you do not have, consider taking out a policy to cover you for any future legal problems – the premiums are modest, around 50 euros a year, and often provide a free advice line, and within certain limitations will fund the cost of bringing or defending a claim in court. If you do not have legal expenses cover then contact one of the tenants' associations listed below for free initial advice. You can also avoid expensive litigation by asking to use the free voluntary conciliation procedure (*la conciliation judiciaire*) provided by the French legal system. This is initiated by writing to *le greffe du Tribunal d'Instance* explaining the issues in dispute. The judge will invite both the tenant and the landlord to put their cases in writing and will then provide them with a considered opinion. This procedure does not bind tenant or landlord, but it can encourage the achievement of an agreement without incurring legal costs.

The tenant's right of first refusal (*le droit de préemption*).

A landlord who wants to sell residential premises let on a long-term basis is obliged to offer the property to the tenant. Landlords are required to notify the tenant in writing of the sale price, and other conditions of sale. Should the landlord not do this, the tenant can challenge the sale and buy the property for the price at which the landlord had tried to sell.

Further information and advice for tenants

L'Agence Nationale pour l'Information sur le Logement – see its website at www.anil.org for useful information for tenants (and landlords).

La Confédération du Logement et du Cadre de Vie (CLCV) www.clcv.org.

L'Association des Comités de Défense des Locataires (ACDL) 11, rue de Bellefond, 75009 Paris (01 48 74 94 84).

For local advice see L'Association Départementale pour l'Information sur le Logement (ADIL) listed in *Les Pages Blanches* under ADIL.

BUYING A PROPERTY ON THE RIVIERA

There are considerable price differentials across the Côte d'Azur. Not surprisingly property is more expensive along the coast. Those who are prepared to purchase further inland can obtain a quite substantial villa with a pool, for the same price as a small flat in the popular coastal resorts.

The most expensive properties are to be found along the coast in Cannes (also the area known as Californie), Saint Tropez, Cap d'Antibes, St Jean-Cap Ferrat, Eze, Cap d'Ail, Roquebrune-Cap Martin, Villeneuve-Loubet and Beaulieu-sur-Mer. The attractive town of Menton is less expensive, but nevertheless is very popular, and is conveniently located for easy access to the Isola ski resort. Mougins and Valbonne are also very pleasant, and property prices are not as high as in the more prestigious areas, though these two towns are particularly popular with the British and other foreigners, partly because of the proximity of the Sophia Antipolis technology park. Prices are lower again in places such as Cagnes-sur-Mer and Saint Laurent-du-Var. Better value properties can also be found in and around Grasse, the perfume capital of France.

The terrain from Nice eastwards to the Italian border is generally not suited for construction as there is very little flat land. Gardens along this part of the coast tend to be pretty steep. The land is flatter to the west of Nice. The town of Mouans-Sartoux, in particular, has good facilities, including a cinema with plenty of free parking.

Prices are considerably lower as you move westwards into the Var, with Saint Tropez being a notable exception. As you travel west along the A8 motorway you cannot help but notice the contrast between the built up coastal areas of the Alpes-Maritimes, and the open spaces, forests and fresh air of the Var. Lac St. Cassien is only ten minutes or so from the A8 motorway junction – one of the restaurants on the lake, Les Arbousiers, was once used by Jaguar to hold a reception for the press, with guests test-driving vehicles on the motorway journey from the airport to the restaurant. Les Adrets (meaning the southern and sunny side of a mountain) is only a short drive from the A8. Montauroux and Fayence are also worth visiting.

New builds

There are a number of reputable house builders carrying out new projects on the Côte d'Azur, including developers such as George V and Kaufman Broad and Marignan. There remains a massive shortage of new properties – owing to restrictions imposed by local authorities. Only around 3,000 new properties are currently being built each year, with demand for new homes exceeding supply. Property prices have risen consistently in the region for the past six years, providing a good long-term return for those who have invested in property.

Finding a suitable property

In searching for property to purchase you are not short of available assistance, with the Côte d'Azur boasting nearly 4,000 estate agents and nearly 1,000 websites to browse through! Publications that are worth consulting include *Nice-Matin Immobilier, Soleil Immobilier, Mag Immo, Indicateur Bertrand Grand Sud,* and *Residence Immobilier Côte d'Azur.* The latter retails at 7.60 euros, but is often available at distribution units at Nice airport free of charge. If you are short of time it is worthwhile using a relocation agency. Estate Net France Sarl (www.est8net.com), for example, will arrange inspection flights to cover a period of 3–4 days, during which you will be shown around a selection of properties in your chosen area. A charge of 199 euros is made, with Estate Net France meeting the balance of the cost of your visit.

Jackie Pressman who runs French Riviera Property Search (www.frenchrivierapropertysearch.com) also finds properties for clients to buy or rent, negotiates on their behalf with vendors or landlords and their representatives, and can put you in contact with English speaking professionals to provide additional services such as accountants, insurers, surveyors, etc.

Jane Copeland at France Rentals also assists those seeking to purchase or rent on the Côte d'Azur. (www.francerentals.co.uk; email jane@francerentals.co.uk)

I strongly recommend that anyone intending to purchase a property in France should obtain advice from their own professional advisers before committing themselves. You will find more detailed information and advice about buying property in France in the latest edition of my book *The Complete Guide to Buying Property in France* (2006), Kogan Page, ISBN 0749444193 and in *Buying a Property in France* by Clive Kristen (2002), HowToBooks, ISBN 1 85703 769 3. The following general principles should be followed by all prospective purchasers:

1. **Instruct your own lawyer**. French *notaires* are publicly appointed officials whose primary responsibilities consist of drafting legal documents, ensuring that the transfer is properly recorded, and ensuring that the parties pay the correct tax. They do not undertake the services traditionally carried out by the UK solicitor, most notably the pre-contract enquiries. In addition whilst many *notaires* speak some English, relatively few are sufficiently skilled in the language to fully communicate with you on complex issues. Importantly, your purchase of a property in France can have consequences for your tax liabilities in the

UK and for the distribution of your estate on your death. Accordingly I recommend instructing either a lawyer, or a team of lawyers, who have an understanding of the relevant laws of *both* systems. There are a number of UK firms of solicitors that provide such a service, including Tee France (www.teefrance.co.uk; 01279 755 200) for whom I act as a consultant and who have their own French *avocat* on board. You should instruct a lawyer well before you commit yourself to a purchase, and ideally at the early stages of making your plans.

2. **Familiarise yourself with the area in which you wish to purchase.** Remember that an area may be very different during the winter months from the snapshot one sees in summer, in terms of its climate, the people living there and the availability of local facilities. Some areas are subject to natural afflictions such as flooding, or termites. If you have decided on such an area then particular care is required in your choice of property.

3. **Always inspect the property yourself, preferably several times.** Ask the vendors and their agents why they are wanting to sell. Endeavour to speak to the neighbours. Is there anything to suggest that they are likely to be 'neighbours from hell' who should be avoided at all cost? Is there anything about the property that could cause problems in the future, such as a well-worn pathway that might suggest a right-of-way over the property, or a stream that might overflow in heavy rain?

4. **Instruct a surveyor** to inspect the property and prepare a report; provide them with a list of any concerns you may have from your own inspection of the property. A structural survey may well save you from purchasing a property that is structurally unsound and which could prove extremely

expensive to put right. A further reason for obtaining a report is that your surveyor may well identify a collection of minor or perhaps more significant defects that though not putting you off, will furnish you with arguments to negotiate on the price.

5. **Do not be tempted to declare at an undervalued price**. The French authorities are enforcing the law and can impose severe penalties on both buyer and seller where they find the value of a property has been under declared.

6. **Do not expect to make a quick, short-term capital gain.** It is best to assume that it will take several years before you could make any significant net gain on a sale.

3
Finding a job

WORKING AT HOME AND LONG-DISTANCE COMMUTING

Modern technology and low cost flights to France's second airport have enabled a considerable number of Britons to move to the Riviera, while still retaining employment or running a business in the UK. Modern technology permits them to carry out far more work at home than was possible ten or 20 years ago, and economical flights facilitate regular trips back to the UK. Others cram their working week into four days, rent a room in a house in London and fly back to their French home for a long weekend with their family.

Indeed, the marketing director of easyJet France told *Nice-Matin* that she believes that a number of her company's passengers commute on a *daily* basis. The hour's time difference means that if you take an 08.00 flight from Nice (with British Airways) you can be in Heathrow by 09.10, and depending on the location of your workplace, at your desk by 10.00 or thereabouts. Much depends on your final destination in the UK.

This trend is also evidenced by a change in the profile of the British now moving to the Côte d'Azur – they are younger, in the job market and generally less wealthy than their compatriots who have moved there in previous years.

If you are working in the UK but are resident in France, returning to your family at weekends and holidays, you should request an E106 which will cover you and your family for health care in France. On the other hand, if your family is living in France, but you are employed and resident in the UK, and only returning to your family every few months, then the appropriate E-form is the E109, which will cover your dependants in France.

WORKING IN FRANCE FOR A UK EMPLOYER

If you are sent to work in France by a UK employer on a temporary basis you will generally remain under the UK system of taxation and National Insurance. Your tax and National Insurance contributions will be deducted from your salary by your UK employer in the usual way. Whilst you will be subject to French income tax, you will receive credit for the tax paid in the UK and there should normally be no additional tax liability to the French authorities. You should, however, make an annual tax declaration in France, which for 2006 had to be completed by the end of May, though hitherto the deadline was the end of March. You should receive an E101 to establish your entitlement to the same social security and health benefits as French citizens, in particular partial reimbursement of health costs. You should consider taking out medical insurance (*une mutuelle*) to cover, for example, the cost of post-operative outpatient care which can be expensive and which is no longer fully covered under the French state system.

Your employer will have to apply for a fresh E101 each year. The French authorities are not keen on granting more than one twelve month extension, though they have been known to make several extensions up to a total of five years.

The above also applies to those who are self-employed in the UK but are working temporarily in France.

FINDING A JOB ON THE RIVIERA

Whilst the unemployment rate in the Alpes-Maritimes is certainly higher than the UK, there are numerous English speakers and other foreigners working here.

Where to find a job

Those seeking to find employment on the Riviera should make use of the various publications, websites and practical assistance (such as access to the internet, a photocopier, telephones, computers, reference books and company listings) provided by European and national bodies such as the EURES and the French ANPE (for local offices of these French job centres see under *Administration du Travail et de l'Emploi* in the Yellow Pages or *Pages Jaunes*. EURES (European Employment Services) was set up by the European Commission to provide a network to liaise with the various national member states' employment services to facilitate the free movement of labour, partly by identifying labour shortages and by encouraging and assisting Europeans to move within Europe for employment. You should look at the websites www.eures-jobs.com and www.europa.eu.int/jobs/eures and make contact with your local EURES adviser in the UK before leaving

34

(through your local Job Centre) and/or on the Côte d'Azur (through ANPE) both before leaving and on arrival. Those jobs advertised on the websites that have a blue flag are jobs for which the employers have expressed an interest in employing workers from other EU member states.

As an EU citizen you are entitled to the same level of advice and assistance from ANPE as a French citizen. At your first interview at the ANPE you will be required to prepare a *Projet d'Action Personalisé (PAP)* with an ANPE adviser. National employment agencies websites that are worth consulting include: www.adecco.fr; www.adia.fr; www.apec.asso.fr; www.cadresonline.com; www.rebondir.fr; www.emploi.org; www.action-emploi.net; www.emploiregions.com and www.manpower.fr. You should also take a look at the websites of the British Chamber of Commerce www.bccriviera.com, Riviera Radio www.rivieraradio.mc, the French Riviera pages of www.angloinfo.com and *Nice-Matin* www.nice-matin.fr. National publications that may also carry some job advertisements for the region include *Le Figaro* (Mondays), *Le Monde* (Mondays and Tuesdays) and *Carrières et Emplois* (Wednesdays).

Teaching positions

Whilst there are quite a few British in the region teaching English as a foreign language (see under *Cours de Langues* in *Les Pages Jaunes*), there are relatively few positions for teachers. The best course of action would be to keep a vigilant eye on the various British and International schools' websites (see Chapter 8), and to send a well-prepared unsolicited letter and CV to each of the schools. Do not be surprised if you do not receive a reply. You may also find positions advertised in the *Times Educational Supplement* (www.tesjobs.co.uk) or at www.ecis.org, the website for the

European Council of International Schools.

Do not assume that because you speak fluent English you will walk into a job as a teacher of English as a foreign language, or even be able to obtain private lessons. There are very few native English speakers employed to teach English in French schools. Furthermore, as far as private lessons to school children are concerned, parents want teachers who can help teach their children the English that they learn in school. The teaching method adopted in schools is generally very dry, and centred around learning grammatical rules in a way that most native English-speakers never learn. Whilst parents would be thrilled at the prospect of their child speaking English with ease, they will generally prefer to instruct a French person who is used to teaching English as it is taught in French schools, with the immediate objective of achieving success at school. Fully qualified teachers are obviously at an advantage over those without teaching qualifications, as are those with a TEFL (Teaching English as a Foreign Language) qualification.

Employment opportunities

On the Riviera there is a particular demand for employees to work in:

- the high-tech sector
- tourism;
- security services;
- gardening and maintenance;
- the yachting industry;
- childcare;
- domestic service.

Unskilled workers on the French Riviera are at a distinct disadvantage owing to the influx of large numbers of economic migrants from Portugal, Spain and North Africa looking for unskilled work, though in some cases employers like their staff to be able to speak English. Accordingly this can give native English-speakers the edge, though usually only if they also speak reasonably good French.

The high-tech sector

The high-tech sector on the Riviera has now overtaken tourism as a source of income and jobs. Over 1,000 businesses employ around 30,000 staff, many in research and development, and especially in information technology and life sciences. There are now large numbers of foreign businesses playing a significant role in the local economy, concentrated in Nice and Sophia Antipolis. The Sophia Antipolis Technology Park, created in 1969 and contributed to by the towns of Biot, Valbonne, Mougins, Vallauris, Antibes, Villeneuve-Loubet, La Colle-sur-Loup, Opio and Roquefort-les-Pins, covers over 2,300 hectares and is the largest of its kind in Europe. Details of the companies, the type of work they carry out and the number of employees can be obtained from the Sophia Antipolis website www.sophia-antipolis.org (go to *Liste des Entreprises* or click on the Union Jack and The Companies). They include:

- Amadeus (employing around 1,200 people, website www.amadeus.com);

- Dow Agrosciences;

- SmithKline Beecham Clinical Laboratories;

- Allergan Europe;

- IBM;

- Texas Instruments;

- Philips Semiconductors;

- Schneider Electric;

- Symag;

- Thales Underwater Systems;

- Intel.

Other companies with a base on the Côte d'Azur include:

- Pricewaterhouse Coopers;

- Adecco;

- Kone;

- Alcatel (Cannes).

The Nice Côte d'Azur Chamber of Commerce regularly publishes a magazine entitled *Azur Entreprises* that is well worth reading. Information is also available on their website www.ccinice-cote-azur.com.

The technology park is also home to numerous educational establishments, including a substantial number of higher education institutions such as:

- University of Nice-Sophia-Antipolis;

- the CERAM centre of education and applied management;

- CERAMICS – a research institute in computer science and applied technology;

- CRESPA which specialises in accountancy, banking, computing, human resources, marketing, insurance and tourism and various language centres.

The park is also home to numerous consultancy agencies covering a wide range of disciplines such as marketing, human relations and industrial property.

One disadvantage of living and working in Sophia Antipolis (or Sophia as it is often known) is the traffic congestion in the morning and at the end of the working day. For newcomers this is only made worse by the inadequacy of street signs – a major problem in an area that to the uninitiated resembles a huge maze or a network of rabbit warrens. Public transport provision is poor and the cost of housing is high.

The Sophia Antipolis website www.sophia-antipolis.org contains a wide range of business and practical information in English. The information includes summaries and contact details for numerous associations and community groups, covering science activities, sports, art, culture, theatre, animal welfare and various other pressure groups, Christian groups, etc.

The park even has its own radio station: *Clin d'Oeil FM* – ALMA Radio (FM106.1), Les Boulides, c/o CIV, 190 rue Frederick Mistral, BP 97 06902 Sophia Antipolis, Cedex. (04 93 65 25 04). At www.sophianet-teleavision.com you will find a selection of videos covering the history and important conferences and other events relating to Sophia.

There is a Sophia Antipolis Association (for membership 04 92 96 78 00, or email info@sophia-antipolis.org) that welcomes newcomers and produces a monthly newspaper *Nouvelles de Sophia*. Another organisation is AHPSA. (Association des Habitants du Parc de Sophia Antipolis www.ahpsa.com; 04 92 96 04 91).

Jobs in businesses serving English-speaking expatriates

Many of those British who go to the Riviera to work, or in search of work, find employment in businesses that primarily serve the English speaking or international communities living there, taking jobs as:

- teachers in the international schools;
- employees of estate agencies, letting agencies and banks;
- yachting industry support staff;
- domestic staff;
- security guards;
- chauffeurs;
- gardeners;
- property maintenance staff.

The Fleurs de Provence Agency is frequently looking for recruits for positions as gardeners, cleaners, nannies and housekeepers, as well as employees who can carry out a range of household repairs or maintenance tasks (www.fleursdeprovence.com; 04 93 34 60 73). Oasis Services also regularly recruits both permanent and temporary staff. You can send a CV to oasisservices@wanadoo.fr or telephone 04 93 65 61 23.

Driving

There are many drivers employed along the coast by car hire companies to drop off and collect vehicles, and also to work as chauffeurs of luxury cars. In both cases applicants generally need to have had a driving licence for at least two years. A good local knowledge and a smart appearance are essential. You can find lists of potential employers under *Location de voiture de luxe* in the *Les Pages Jaunes*.

Yachting

Agencies that recruit for the yachting industry on the French Riviera include: Fred Dovaston (www.yachtjob.com), YPI Crew (04 92 90 46 10), Camper and Nicholson (www.cnconnect.com), Viking Recruitment (www.Vikingrecruitment.com) and www.yachtingpages.com. You can pick up a (free) copy of the Yachting Pages Marine Directory from Geoffrey's of London in Antibes or by telephoning 04 93 34 35 34. Positions on yachts are often advertised on *Riviera Radio* or on its website www.rivieraradio.mc.

Banks and insurance

Banks and insurance companies require considerable numbers of summer staff. Here again, if the opportunity to impress and to make personal contacts is taken, there may be prospects of obtaining a permanent post. It is worthwhile contacting L'Association Pour L'Emploi dans les Societes d'Assurance (APESA) as it coordinates job offers throughout France. Applicants need to be aged at least 18 and have had three months' experience in the sector (see its website www.emploi-assurance.com). Banks are particularly keen to recruit those with some experience. BNP Paribas for example is a major recruiter. Applications should be made in January for summer posts.

Teaching English

Rates for teaching English, if you are successful in obtaining the work, are a modest 10–20 euros an hour in most cases.

Work with French employers

French employers seem a little wary of taking on British staff, and if you do not speak much French your prospects are not good. There are, however, some British who manage to obtain positions with French employers, and some who succeed in gaining promotion. They generally have a good knowledge of written and spoken French, and a willingness to adapt.

If you speak French fluently and have experience as well as qualifications in Information Technology then you will find it much easier to obtain employment than in other sectors. There is an IT skill shortage in France, partly caused by the large numbers of young French people with these skills leaving France to work in London.

Miscellaneous

Those with a good knowledge of Italian are also well-placed to find work in many sectors.

Note that there are various schemes to help the unemployed get back to work. These schemes include a tax-free subsidy of up to nearly 2,000 euros if you are taken on for a permanent position (or a contract of at least 12 months) and have to travel over 25 km from your home, or have a journey of more than one hour.

Distributors of publicity material are poorly paid, but it is work that can often be fitted around other responsibilities. It is generally necessary to have a car, and applicants must be over 18. You will find a list of employers in the Yellow Pages under *'Distribution d'imprimes'*.

You can find lists of companies and their details at: www.kompass.fr, www.bottin.fr, www.europages.com, www.euridile.inpi.fr and www.regionsjob.com.

TAX AND SOCIAL SECURITY CONTRIBUTIONS

Most of these are paid by the employer. This nevertheless leaves employees paying up to 13.6% of their salary in contributions. These are, however, deductible for the purposes of assessing your liability to pay income tax. French income tax is fairly complex, though once you have mastered the concept of *le quotient familial* you are halfway there. In brief, the taxable income of a household is divided into a number of parts depending on the marital status of the couple and the number of their dependants. Those with no children or other dependants pay rather more of their income in tax than those with a family. Those who are unmarried but have registered a PACS (*Le Pacte Civil de Solidarité* – the French equivalent to a civil partnership, see Chapter 7) are entitled to make a joint tax declaration in the same way as married couples. If you are simply living together and are not married and have not entered into a PACS then you are required to make separate tax returns. Everyone should complete and file a tax declaration by the notified deadline (for 2006 the date limit for this was 31st May, with further time for those completing their declaration by internet).

USEFUL WEBSITES

Useful websites include: www.anpe.fr, www.apecita.com, www.jobpilot.fr, www.emailjob.com, www.directemploi.com, www.forum-emplois.com, www.emploi.org, www.action-emploi.net, www.monster.fr and www.jobalacarte.com.

ANPE OFFICES

Antibes: Quartier Nova Antipolis, 665 premiere avenue. (04 93 74 01 30)

Cannes: 158, rue d'Antibes. (04 92 18 83 30)

Cannes (Hotellerie-Restauration): 99 av Georges Clemenceau. (04 93 99 23 80)

Nice centre (there are 8 different offices within Nice): 10, rue Oscar II. (04 93 97 90 00)

Valbonne: Point Emploi – Mairie Annexe, 26 rue Vigne Haute. (04 93 00 34 24)

WORKING FROM HOME

A substantial proportion of home workers are engaged in **telemarketing**. The numbers of British and other foreigners with a good level of spoken English means that there is now a demand for fluent English speakers to work in telemarketing in France, at least those with a high level of French. You can obtain further information from the Syndicat du marketing telephonique et medias electroniques, 26 rue des Rigoles, 75020 Paris. (0892 68 68 72)

Other home workers carry out public opinion polls over the telephone. One advantage of this work is that it can be fitted around family or other responsibilities. You can find more information on www.sofres.fr; www.ipsos.com; www.bva.fr.

National websites providing information on employee rights, access to training courses, etc. include www.travail.gouv.fr and www.emploi-solidarite.gouv.fr.

CONTRACTS OF EMPLOYMENT

Contracts of employment must be of either indeterminate duration (*contrats à durée indeterminée* or *CDI*) or for fixed periods of up to nine months (*contrats à durée determinée* or *CDD*). It is difficult for employers to terminate a *CDI* after one month as they are by law required to justify their actions and comply with certain procedural requirements. Temporary contracts, or *CDI*, must be in writing and are only permitted where the contract is genuinely for a temporary post, or to replace a person on maternity leave, for example. If the contract is oral, or in writing but fails to state the reason why the employment is for a limited period, then the law deems that the employment is on a permanent contract.

There are a number of exceptions to the above basic rules which are aimed at encouraging employers to take on certain categories of workers, such as those undergoing training, new entrants to the job market, the long-term unemployed and genuine seasonal workers.

PAY AND HOURS

At the time of writing the minimum wage in France, or *le Smic,* is around 1,150 euros a month for a 35-hour week (7.61 euros an hour). Semi-skilled workers have a minimum wage 25% above this level, and skilled workers 50% more.

The 35-hour week introduced only a few years ago has recently been substantially relaxed as it was causing many problems for employers in terms of productivity and staff availability. Employers are now entitled to require employees to work up to 200 additional hours per year. Employees may, if they wish, work more hours than this, though they may not normally work for more than ten hours a day, or for more than six days a week.

DISMISSAL

Before an employer can dismiss an employee they must invite them to attend an interview. This invitation should be sent by registered letter and give at least five days' notice so that the employee can take advice and arrange for someone to accompany them to the interview. The employer must state their reasons for being dissatisfied with the employee, and listen to any explanation. If they decide to dismiss the employee, they must do so by registered letter giving their reasons for deciding upon dismissal. The dismissed employee then has the right to appeal to *Le Conseil des Prud'hommes*, a court equivalent to the UK Employment Tribunal. The *Conseil* can order reinstatement and payment of damages by the employer.

LE CHÈQUE EMPLOI SERVICE

This was introduced to simplify the administrative procedures for the employment of domestic employees, gardeners and those who look after or educate children in their employer's home. It applies only when a person works for no more than eight hours a week for any one employer. The employee must not work more than a total of 40 hours per week.

Instead of a contract of employment and pay slip the employer obtains a 'chequebook' from their bank or from a post office. They then fill out a form and forward this to the *Centre National de Traitement de Chèque Emploi Service* or *CNTCES* together with bank details. The security contributions for the employee are then deducted from the employer's bank account by the *CNTCES*. Each time a payment is due the employer completes the 'cheque' to the employee at the same time sending a notification to the *CNTCES*. The *CNTCES* will then send a pay slip to the employee. Using this system enables the employer to claim a reduction in their personal tax bill of up to 50% of the amount paid to the employee, and possibly a reduction in their liability to pay social contributions.

I have included substantial further detail on contracts of employment and employee rights (such as holidays, maternity and paternity leave, discrimination, etc.) in my book *The Tee France Guide to Living and Working in France* (2006) available on www.amazon.co.uk.

Other useful websites on taxation and employment legislation include: www.impots.gouv.fr; www.travail.gouv.fr; www.emploi-solidarite.gouv.fr.

SETTING UP A BUSINESS

A considerable number of expatriates start their own business on the Riviera, ranging from hairdressing to offering insurance and financial advice to expatriates. An invaluable source of information for those in business, or those contemplating going into business is the local British Chamber of Commerce (see its website www.bccriviera.org).

The first point to bear in mind before setting up a business is that despite much recent simplification, and even ignoring the fact that you will be operating partially at least in a foreign language, starting a business in France is more complicated than in the UK.

Secondly, businesses generally face considerable tax and National Insurance bills after they have been operating for two or three years. These can suddenly become crippling, especially if profits increase rapidly and then fall a little, even if the long-term outlook is good. Generally tax and National Insurance are easier to pay when profits are steadily rising, rather than if they fluctuate – even if the long-term trend is upwards.

The difficulties with establishing and running a business in France have led many people to work illegally, or to employ illegal workers. The consequences of this if you are discovered by the tax authorities are serious – fines of up to 30,000 euros. Indeed the punishments available to the courts include a term of imprisonment. Whilst the employee is also committing a crime, the authorities take a more severe stance against offending employers. Any employer who does break the rules is always at risk of a disgruntled employee or client making an anonymous call to the tax authorities.

Help and advice

There is a wide range of sources of advice and practical and financial assistance. It is worth consulting the French Embassy website (www.ambafrance.org.co.uk) and the French Chamber of Commerce (www.ccfgb.co.uk) in the UK. In France you should consider making contact with L'Association pour le Développement de l'Initiative Economique (www.adie.org), Le Banque de Développement des Petites et Moyennes Entreprises (www.bdpme.fr), L'Agence Pour la Création d'Entreprise (www.apce.com) and L'Agence Nationale Pour L'Emploi (www.anpe.fr). The first three organisations provide financial loans and bank guarantees, the fourth arranges workshops, advice sessions and free courses in French for foreigners. It is also worth researching the website www.subsidies-in-france.com. Women should take a look at www.droit-femmes.gouv.fr, the website of the Fonds de Garantie à l'Initiative des Femmes which offers loans and guarantees to women intending to start businesses. Those over 50 should investigate the possibility of finance in the form of an interest free loan from EDEN (Encouragement au Développement des Entreprises Nouvelles).

On the Côte d'Azur you should seriously consider networking with other English speakers in business in the area. As suggested before, do take a look at the website of the local British chamber of commerce (www.bccriviera.com) and the activities run by the chamber. Members are entitled to use the BCC logo on all their documents and advertising material, to receive a free copy of the *Riviera Times,* participation in a discounted travel insurance scheme, and reduced rates for all BCC events (see www.bccriviera.org).

Other sources include the Nice Côte d'Azur Chamber of Commerce that has a useful resource centre (Chambre de Commerce et d'Industrie Nice Côte d'Azur, 20 boulevard Carabacel BP 1259, 06005 Nice Cedex 1; 0820 42 22 22; email crca@cote-azur.cci.fr). You can obtain help and advice from the Chamber before you arrive in France. They will welcome you on any fact-finding trips you wish to make and generally facilitate the establishment of your business. The Chamber's website is partially in English (see www.ccinice-cotedazur.com and click on the Union Jack), though the most useful information is in French only under *Espace Enterprises – service aux entreprises* (see left hand side of screen, or go straight to www.cci-service-entreprises.com/accueil). There are also seven local *Maisons d'Entreprise* in the department of Les Alpes-Maritimes in:

- Antibes;

- Cannes;

- Grasse;

- Menton;

- Nice;

- Plaine-du-Var;

- Sophia Antipolis.

The addresses of the *Maisons d'Entreprise* can be obtained from the Yellow Pages or from the website of the Nice Côte d'Azur Chamber of Commerce (see above).

Centre de Formalités des Entreprises (CFE)

You will need to register with your local CFE where you will be advised of the importance of having a business number (SIRET) – in brief you should not start trading before you receive this, and should have the number on all business stationery. Your local French Chamber of Commerce will advise you of the location of the nearest appropriate CFE.

Starting a business in Sophia Antipolis

It is well worth consulting the website www.sophia-antipolis.net/uk. This includes information on:

- how to set up a business in Sophia Antipolis;
- administrative procedures and financial assistance;
- advice on start up (with a link to the Start Up Club www.sophia-startup.com);
- how to obtain access to venture capital;
- links to the Côte d'Azur Hi Tech Club, the Institut Eurocom, and the International Venture Capital Summit (IVCS), and around ten business centres in the park.

The Start Up Club

The Start Up Club is an association that seeks to encourage people from a wide range of backgrounds (scientists, students, teachers, engineers, researchers, representatives of financial institutions and local authorities) to meet to discuss and share ideas with a view to encouraging the dissemination of information and the creation of new projects.

Banks and businesses

Of the various banks operating along the coast, the Banque Populaire Côte d'Azur is particularly keen to attract British business clients and has several pages of its website in English (www.cotedazur.banquepopulaire.fr – see flag at extreme bottom left hand corner). See also www.businessriviera.com (click on the Union Jack towards the top right hand corner for pages in English).

If you wish to obtain finance, whether from a government agency, or a private bank, you will need to produce a well-argued and well-presented business plan.

Business structures

There are a number of different forms that your business could take. The most popular amongst the British in business on the Côte d'Azur is the *Entreprise Individuelle* or sole trader. This is easy to set up. Those contemplating doing so should consult a *notaire* with a view to making a *déclaration d'insaisissabilité,* a new innovation that enables you to protect your home from creditors. You should also take advice on your *régime matrimonial – la séparation des biens* is generally the most appropriate as this will protect your spouse's assets from your creditors should the business fail.

The second most popular business vehicle is the limited liability company or *La Société à Responsabilité Limitée* (*SARL*). This requires two shareholders, though you can form a one shareholder only limited company (*L'Entreprise Unipersonelle à Responsabilité Limitée* or *EURL*). Further details of the above, and other possible vehicles with which to operate a business, and the various options in relation to the taxation of businesses can be found in my book *The Tee Guide to Living and Working in France* and also in *Starting a Business in France* by Richard Whiting, published by How To Books.

Working with your spouse or partner

This is so often how new businesses become established. It is important, however, that you should both discuss with a legal adviser and/or accountant how the business is to be run, so that you both are fully aware of the different options available. Your spouse could be a shareholder if the business is operated as a *SARL* (*conjoint associé*), or an employee (*conjoint salarié*). Another option, available where you operate as a sole trade or one shareholder limited company, is that of *conjoint collaborateur.* The spouse receives no payment, but is entitled to health benefits and if appropriate, maternity benefits. After ten years working as a *conjoint collaborateur* the spouse becomes entitled to a capital sum and pension entitlement on the death of the sole trader or owner of the single shareholder company. No inheritance tax is payable on this sum.

Franchises

If you are contemplating opening a franchise you might wish to contact INFORM, a business in Nice (57, rue Canta Galet 06200 Nice) that advises both franchisers and franchisees. The failure rate of new franchise businesses is less than a third of that for new businesses generally, partly because of the guidance provided by the franchisor who will usually want the franchisee to succeed.

UK UNEMPLOYMENT BENEFIT

If you have been out of work in the UK you can have Jobseeker's Allowance paid to you in France for a period of up to 13 weeks. To benefit you must be registered as a job seeker for no less than four weeks before leaving the UK, and be available for work up until your departure. You are required to register with the French authorities within seven days of your last claim for Jobseeker's Allowance in the UK. You must make contact with your Jobcentre Plus office or Jobcentre before your departure, and complete the appropriate forms in order to claim benefit. You should be sent a copy of E303 before you leave to enable you to claim benefit in France, and form E119 to entitle you to health care. If you cannot find employment during that 13-week period, then you will have to return to the UK if you wish to continue to receive benefit. For further information ask for leaflet JSAL 22 available from your local Department of Work and Pensions office.

4
Finding a summer job

A STEP TOWARDS PERMANENT EMPLOYMENT

The important thing to remember here is that a temporary, seasonal job *could* be the most successful route to securing a more permanent position.

In the summer months there is a major shortage of labour. Vacancies consist of two types:

* jobs that only exist in the summer;

* positions that are temporary because permanent workers are on holiday.

In relation to the latter, staff appointed on a temporary basis and who impress their employer may well find that they are offered a permanent position either after the temporary post comes to an end, or at some subsequent point.

JOB FAIRS

Information about seasonal employment on the Côte d'Azur can be found on the website of L'Observatoire Régional des Métiers: www.orm-paca.org. Each year a number of communes hold job fairs for summer posts, including Cannes, Le Cannet and Mandelieu. These frequently take place quite early in the year, such as that for Cannes entitled '*Cet été on bosse*' that took place in February 2006. Employers participating include businesses like Club Med that regularly recruits around 1,700 summer staff in France on contracts of three to six months duration. Other companies taking part include retail chains like Darty or Géant.

All the town councils along the coast recruit summer staff, including workers to police the beaches, with the Ville de Cannes alone recruiting in the region of 300 such staff annually.

LEISURE INDUSTRY OPPORTUNITIES

For those in search of a temporary job in a hotel, or in a restaurant, the prospects are good. An estimated 300,000 extra temporary employees are recruited on the Côte d'Azur each summer to help welcome the millions of tourists who arrive annually. The pay is low, the hours are long and frequently unsocial and accommodation costs in the region are high. Often food is provided – employers of hotel staff receiving the SMIC or minimum wage must provide them with two meals a day, or an extra payment in lieu. Positions available include:

- bar staff;
- dish-washers;
- kitchen hands;

- waiters;
- chambermaids;
- receptionists.

Recruitment can start as early as March.

There is a wide range of other jobs in demand including:

- sports instructors;
- crew and service staff to work on yachts;
- representatives of tour operators;
- shop assistants;
- reception staff;
- campsite, youth hostel, fast food restaurant assistants.

Clearly those who speak well and have a good presentation are at a significant advantage. The ability to speak a foreign language is a definite advantage especially Italian, as is a knowledge of the region.

Beach cafés also hire a considerable number of casual workers, as do businesses that seek to sell food and drinks to tourists by walking along the beaches (*le commerce ambulant*). If you decide to set up your own operation doing this, you will need to register with the appropriate *chambre de métiers* and if you are intending to sell food you will need to make contact with the *DDASS* (the *Direction Départementale des Affaires Sanitaires et Sociales*).

There are also some opportunities to work in the Alpine ski resorts during the winter.

WHERE TO LOOK FOR JOBS

There are a number of useful websites on which positions are advertised including the French sites www.jobsaison.com, www.adecco.fr, www.jobalacarte.com, www.manpower.fr, www.sun-job.com, www.jobdete.com and www.capcampus.com.

Useful sites aimed particularly at students include www.you-unilver.com and www.studyrama.com. Websites in English that are worth visiting include:

- www.resortjobs.com;
- www.overseasjobs.com;
- www.summerjobs.com;
- www.eurosummerjobs.com.

Sites specific to hotel and restaurant staff are www.soshotellerie.com and www.lechef.com.

Specialist publications for this sector include the *Journal de l'Hôtellerie.*

OTHER OPPORTUNITIES

Conference centres

Cannes and Nice are established conference centres with many organisations holding annual events in these two locations, as well as elsewhere along the coast. It is accordingly worthwhile making enquiries at your local tourist office as to the timing of these events if you wish to work in this area.

Holiday and sporting centres

There are – not surprisingly – many holiday and sporting centres in the area with a high demand for qualified instructors. Your prospects of securing a position are greatly enhanced if you have obtained a relevant qualification such as the *Brevet d'Aptitude aux Fonctions d'Animateur* or *BAFA*. You must be over 17 and undertake a training course lasting at least four weeks. This can cost you up to 900 euros unless you are fortunate enough to obtain funding from the local *Conseil Régional* or the *Direction Régionale Jeunesse et Sport*.

If you want to coach a particular sport or other activity then you need to obtain the *BEES* (*Brevet d'État d'Educateur Sportif*) corresponding to the activity that you want teach, or obtain the more general *Brevet Professionnel de la Jeunesse, de l'Education Populaire et du Sport*. *ODEL* (*Office départemental d'éducation et de loisirs*) is a major recruiter of sports instructors for summer courses (see www.odelvar.asso.fr), as is Club Med (08 25 35 25 25 25).

In addition to instructors, holiday centres require a range of ancillary staff, including paramedics. Those who have completed a part of their medical or nursing training, even if only the first year, are well placed to obtain appointments as *assistants sanitaires*.

If you are seriously contemplating working in a holiday centre take a look at the website of the L'Union Nationale des Centres Sportifs de Plein Air (www.ucpa.com). The site contains a number of job offers under the heading 'Recrutement'. Other sites on which job offers are located include www.animjobs.com, www.zanimateurs-fous.com and www.clubmed-jobs.com.

L'APPASCAM (Association pour la Promotion et la

Professionnalisation de l'Animation Sportive et Culturelle dans les Alpes-Maritimes) gives grants to assist people to obtain employment in sport and adventure centres. Their address is 2, rue de la Faux, Résidence le Grand Large – Bât le Galon 1 – 06800 Cagnes-sur-Mer. (04 92 13 79 79; email appascam@wanadoo.fr) There is a similar organisation for the Var: APSA 83, Maison des Sports, Immeuble Helianthe, 83000 Toulon (04 94 93 09 65).

Children's activity events

Local *mairies* frequently organise activities for local children during school holidays, and it is worthwhile finding out whether they have any vacancies.

Hospitals and nursing homes

Of course, for hospitals in the area the busiest summer months coincide with the time when most staff wish to take annual leave. Accordingly there is a substantial summer demand for all levels of hospital staff including porters, cleaners and maintenance employees.

For details of positions available see www.quickmedicalservice.fr and www.appelmedical.com. Private clinics and retirement homes also need staff during the summer period, both for caring for patients and residents but also to work in the kitchens and laundry and to carry out routine cleaning and maintenance.

Autoroute toll booths

Another major employer that faces temporary labour shortages over the summer is Escota that needs staff to man its motorway toll booths. Prospective candidates should write to Le Service du Personnel, RN202, Quartier St. Isidore, 06000 Nice. (04 93 29 85 91) You can consult its website at www.escota.fr.

National employers

Supermarket chains such as Carrefour, La Poste (La Poste, Direction des Alpes-Maritimes, 41 rue Gounod, 06000 Nice (04 93 16 38 00) and SNCF (see its website www.recrutement-sncf.com) also recruit on a large scale. Carrefour, for example, needs staff prepared to start at 05.00 and others to work up to 22.00 or 22.30. France Telecom recruits for its telephone information and customer care services, and also sales staff for its retail outlets. You should send your CV to the head of human resources (*Le Directeur des resources humaines*) of the PACA region in April.

Insurance companies and banks

Seasonal recruitment for insurance companies is co-ordinated nationwide by the Association Pour l'Emploi dans les Sociétés d'Assurance (APESA), 51 rue Saint Georges, 75009 Paris (01 53 20 43 53) www.emploi-assurance.com. Applicants should be over 18 and have some experience of working in the insurance or similar sector. Jobs are also advertised in specialist journals such as *L'Assurance Française.* If you speak fluent French, then your knowledge of English or other foreign language can be an advantage. Banks also need summer staff and applications should be made to the director of human resources in the bank's regional headquarters (generally in Nice, or Marseille) or the *directeur* of any particular branch at which you hope to work. Banks begin considering applications from as early as January.

Agriculture

The agricultural sector has an acute demand for labour over the summer, though it lasts only for a few weeks during the fruit-picking season. Further information is available from the Association Nationale pour l'Emploi et la Formation en Agriculture, www.anefa.org, and also from the Chambre d'Agriculture des Alpes-Maritimes, Marche d'Interet National (MIN) Fleurs 17, Box 85, 1 route de Grenoble, 06296 Nice Cedex 3 (04 93 18 45 00). Many of those taken on have simply turned up by finding addresses of potential employers in the Yellow Pages under *Agriculture: approvisionnement et collecte, Arboriculture et production de fruits* or *Cooperatives Agricoles.* This is hard manual labour, frequently for over eight hours a day, seven days a week over two weeks. Pay is seldom in excess of 40 euros per day, though to this is added food and accommodation.

Museums and historic buildings

The summer months also see an increased demand for guides to work in the local museums and historical buildings. You can obtain contact details and a list of such buildings from the local tourist offices.

Cleaning and maintenance

Summer sees a shortage of people to carry out gardening, domestic cleaning, and odd jobs. Rates of pay average out at around 7.50

euros an hour gross. Work can often be found by putting up notices in local shop windows, or distributing leaflets advertising your service in the locality.

Companies that clean industrial premises are listed in the Yellow Pages under *Nettoyage*.

Security staff are also required to look after building sites, commercial and residential premises at night time. See under *Gardiennage* in the Yellow Pages. A police check (*extrait de casier judiciaire*) is generally required.

ANPE

The ANPE on the Côte d'Azur and the local *Centre Régional Information Jeunesse* now produce an annual guide book: *Guide des jobs d'été*. This can be obtained from any office of the ANPE in the Alpes-Maritimes (such as one of the Nice offices, 04 93 97 90 00), or the CRIJ d'Azur on 04 93 80 93 93 or from some *Offices de Tourisme*. In addition they have a huge number of information sheets specific to employment in particular sectors such as *Les parcs et loisir d'attractions*, *Vacances Familiales, Les bases de loisirs et de plein air, Les loisirs pour enfants et adolescents,* and *Vacances culturels et sportifs*, to name but a few.

The guide contains information on those sectors where demand for labour is highest, useful addresses, contact details and advice on preparing curricula vitae and *lettres de motivation*.

At the local office of ANPE you will be given an initial interview at which you will be assisted by an ANPE adviser in the construction of your personal action project (*Projet d'Action*

Personalisé or *PAP*). This will set out your objectives and possible workshops, training and assistance that you may need to attain them. At ANPE offices you can make use of the internet, photocopiers and a range of documentation and obtain access to a total of 25 different workshops.

The ANPE has a 24-hour-a-day, seven days a week, interactive telephone service (04 93 97 90 00) that enables you to consult job offers and to obtain practical information. Advisers are available from 09.00 to 16.30 Monday to Thursday and 09.00 to 16.00 on a Friday.

The ANPE also has a special centre devoted to the hotel trade – ANPE Nice Hotellerie-Restauration, 15 avenue Durante 06000 Nice where you can consult *Le journal de l'hôtellerie* and other publications.

Alternatively you can attend the offices of the Centre Régional de Jeunesse (CRJ) at 19 rue Gioffredo in Nice, which is open every weekday from 10.00 to 19.00. Here you will find a wide range of practical information and documentation, including training and working abroad, as well as internet access. The CRJ arranges for recruitment managers from major employers to give presentations, and legal sessions where you can receive free advice from practising *avocats*.

IMPROVING YOUR CHANCES

In many cases, of course, jobs are not advertised at all. Positions can be filled by candidates who just try their luck turning up armed with their CV and offering their labour. Indeed a large proportion of vacancies are filled in this way.

For a considerable number of posts you can increase your prospects of employment by obtaining a relatively simple qualification in first aid, such as the *Attestation de Formation de Premiers Secours* (*L'AFPS*) that can be taken by anyone aged 14 and over. This involves 10–15 hours of courses and costs less than 100 euros. More advanced qualifications include the *Attestation de Formation Complémentaire aux Premier Secours Avec Material* (*L'AFCPSAM*) costing around 200–320 euros and requiring 20 hours of participation, or the *Attestation de Formation Complémentaire aux Premiers Secours sur la Route* (*L'AFCPSSR*) consisting of around 8 hours of courses.

USEFUL GUIDES

There are two extremely useful guides for those contemplating summer work, produced by two of France's main trade unions:

*   *Jobs et saisonniers: vos droits ne sont pas en vacances* published by the Confédération Française Démocratique du Travail, www.cdft.fr;

*   *Ma Saison en Poche* published by the Confédération Générale du Travail www.cgt.fr.

TEMPORARY WORK AGENCIES

These include:

*   Adecco www.adecco.fr;

*   Adia France www.adia.fr;

*   Kelly service www.kellyservice.fr;

- Manpower www.manpower.fr;

- Partinaire www.partinaire.fr;

- Vediorbis www.vediorbis.com.

SEASONAL CONTRACTS OF EMPLOYMENT

A seasonal contract is a *CDD* (*contrat de duration determinée*) suitable for companies that have seasonal variations in their demand for work. It must be in writing, for not longer than eight months, must state the purpose for which it is entered into, and explain why the contract is only seasonal. A seasonal contract of employment carries with it no bonus as is the case with the usual *CDI*.

RECEIVING UK UNEMPLOYMENT BENEFIT WHILST IN FRANCE

See the information at the end of the Chapter 3.

5
Studying on
the Côte d'Azur

UNIVERSITY EDUCATION

University fees for French and other EU citizens are modest, though universities in France are stretched to capacity. The University of Nice-Sophia Antipolis is no exception. As in other French universities there is not much in the way of extra-curricular activities. Many students at Nice-Sophia Antipolis University are locals who have chosen a university that they can attend whilst still living at home. Nevertheless, there are substantial numbers of foreign students at the university. You will find detailed information about the university on its website www.unice.fr, including in English (click on «International» and then «English»). Guidance on financing studies is available from the Union Internationale des Etudiants de France, UNEF, 112 boulevard de la Villette 75019 Paris (see www.unef.fr).

The academic year starts in September and applications need to be submitted by the previous January. Non-French speakers must take a language aptitude test. At the end of two years of study students are awarded the *Diplôme d'Etudes Universitaires Générales* or *DEUG*. From this point courses are more specialised. On completion of a third year a *Licence* is awarded (equivalent to a BA or BSc). Students often go on to study for a *maîtrise* equivalent to a Master of Arts or Master of Science.

Visiting students

It is possible to enrol for up to one academic year at a French university as a visiting student. You should contact the International Relations office at Nice University. There are also a number of European educational programmes organised under the auspices of the European Commission. These include the Erasmus Programme under which students have a 3–12 month stay at a university or other higher education institution of another European country. Students take examinations set by the host institution, and these are recognised by the student's home institution. Financial assistance is available to help with travel costs and higher costs of living, and in some cases language tuition. You can obtain further information from the EU's Gateway to Europe, accessible via www.europe.eu.int/ploteus.

For information on educational and training opportunities throughout Europe see the European Commission's PLOTEUS service (Portal Learning Opportunities Throughout Europe). The website, at www.europa.eu.int/ploteus, includes details of national education and training systems. Additional useful information is to be found at www.euroguidance.org.uk.

The Open University

There are a number of people studying with the Open University in France. The OU co-ordinator for France, Rosemary Pearson, offers advice to students and arranges events at which students can meet each other (01 47 58 53 73; r.pearson@open.ac.uk). The Open University is unable to offer face-to-face tutorials to students in France, though many tutors arrange telephone tutorials instead. Students based in France and elsewhere in continental Europe pay a substantial supplement that makes studying with the OU quite expensive. However, if you or your spouse arc UK tax payers then you will generally not be required to pay this extra amount. You can find further information about courses from the OU website www.open.ac.uk. Details about the Open University Business School can be found at www.oubs.open.ac.uk.

London University External Programme

A number of degrees are available for external candidates with the University of London, including in French, English and Law, and also a joint French and Italian degree.

Other institutes of Higher Education

There are several institutes of higher education based in the Sophia Antipolis business park, in particular in the fields of business management, information technology and science. For a full list see www.sophia-antipolis.net (go to '*développer*' and then '*enseignement supérieur*').

CERAM Sophia Antipolis, European School of Business offers a four-year undergraduate degree in English which covers technology, business and communication. (0820 42 44 44; info-eai@ceram.fr; www.ceram.edu/eaitech)

QUALIFICATIONS EQUIVALENCE

Details of how to establish equivalence for educational qualifications is available at the French network of National Academic Recognition Information Centres (NARICs). See the website: http://www.enic-naric.net.

STUDYING FRENCH ON THE RIVIERA

There are a number of language schools on the Côte d'Azur, with some (such as the Collège International de Cannes, 1 avenue Docteur Alexandre Pascal, Cannes. 04 93 47 39 29) offering short-term residential courses in French. Language schools are listed in the Yellow Pages under *Cours de Langues.*

STUDYING FRENCH IN THE UK

French residents, including English speakers, are eligible for a grant from CROUS, which is responsible for funding studies in the UK (see its website www.crous-nice.fr). Details on UK universities can be found via www.sundaytimes.co.uk/universityguide. Information about a year out can be found at www.gapyear.com and www.yearoutgroup.org.

6
Retiring to the Côte d'Azur

Any citizen of a member state of the European Union, including those who are retired, are entitled to live temporarily or permanently in any other member state, including France. You must ensure that you have an up-to-date British passport. You will need to produce this when paying by cheque or if stopped by the police and, of course, to enter France.

France is one of the most popular destinations for people wishing to spend their retirement abroad, with the Côte d'Azur being the first choice for many. Climate is a major factor in its favour, and whilst housing costs are much higher than elsewhere in France, you can still often obtain better value for money than in many parts of Britain. As elsewhere in France, fuel and travel costs are a little lower than in the UK, and residents in France have the advantage of an efficient and user-friendly health service.

POINTS TO BEAR IN MIND

Those who retire abroad sometimes feel that they are too distant from their family and rather isolated. France is very different from the UK, and often expatriates are surprised by how much they miss their home country. Such feelings can be particularly acute when a person loses their partner, or has problems managing owing to illness or advancing age. One of the advantages of moving to the Côte d'Azur, particularly the Alpes-Maritimes, is the presence of fellow expatriates and services and associations specifically for British residents or English-speakers. This is less true, of course, for those who choose to live in the Var.

France is not particularly well-equipped with care and nursing homes for the elderly, though there are a number of retirement homes on the Côte d'Azur, including one, the Sunnybank Retirement home, catering for English-speakers and due to open its doors in 2007 (see Chapter 9 Health Services for further information).

There are several useful websites that have practical information for the elderly, including directories of retirment homes, with some sites having partial information in English. www.agevillage.com, www.maison-de-retraite.net, and www.arepa.org (the website of L'Association des Résidences pour les Personnes Agées) are all worth consulting, as is the English website www.seniorsworld.co.uk. General advice, is also available from Age Concern, Astral House, 1268 London Road, London SW16 4ER (020 8765 7200).

RECEIVING YOUR PENSION IN FRANCE

You can have your state or private pension paid to you in France. You have the same rights to health care as a French citizen. Note that those wishing to retire early may be able to benefit from health cover up to two and a half years prior to the usual date of retirement. As a retired person you are entitled to full reimbursement of your medical expenses. You should obtain the practical guide – *Your Social Security Rights when moving within the EU* from the website www.europa.eu. Ask the UK Pension Service's International Pension Centre, which is part of the Department for Work and Pensions (DWP), (0191 2187777; www.dwp.gov.uk) to send you a copy of its leaflet SA29 (available online at www.dwp.gov.uk/international/sa29), and form E121. You will need this to enable you to register with the French health services. If you have not yet retired you should ask for form E106. Whether you are retired or not you should register at the local health office (*caisse primaire d'assurance maladie*) where arrangements will be made for you to receive a French medical card.

You can keep up to date with changes in UK pensions (the system is currently undergoing a major overhaul) by visiting www.thepensionservice.gov.uk (00 44 191 218 2828).

One potential difficulty when the source of your income is in the UK, at least until (if ever) the UK adopts the euro, is exchange rate fluctuations. One option is to move some of your investments to France. In any event you should ask your financial adviser about the possibility of doing this, should the value of sterling show signs of declining further against the euro.

APPROACHING RETIREMENT

If you have not yet retired when you move to France, but continue working there, you will have your existing entitlement to a UK pension frozen. When you reach pensionable age you will receive a reduced pension from the UK authorities. If you are nearing retirement age you should consider making voluntary payments to bring your National Insurance contributions up to the level entitling you to a full pension. Contact the Pension Service's International Pension Centre on 0191 218 7777 and the Inland Revenue's Centre for Non-Residents on 0845 070 0040. Ask them to explain the current different costs and benefits of paying Class 2 or Class 3 contributions. The following link will also address many of the relevant questions: www.thepensionservice.gov.uk/atoz/atozdetailed/livingoverseas.asp.

OTHER UK BENEFITS

Most benefits, including invalidity and disability benefits, widows' benefits or benefits received as a result of an accident at work, or an occupational disease, are payable to you (gross) wherever you choose to live. You can only receive incapacity benefit if you have paid Class 1 or Class 2 and 4 National Insurance contributions.

7
Settling on the Côte d'Azur

YOUR RIGHT TO STAY IN FRANCE

As stated elsewhere, all citizens of member states of the European Union have the right to live and work in France.

IMPORTING YOUR BELONGINGS

As an EU citizen you have the right to bring all personal belongings with you to France. Restrictions apply to drugs and firearms, animals, animal products, plants and items with a possible military use. If you are uncertain ask the French customs beforehand.

TAKING AND LOOKING AFTER YOUR PETS

Cats and dogs

If you wish to take your dog or cat to France you must have it identified with a microchip, vaccinated against rabies and issued with a pet passport (in that order). Your name and address, the date the animal was microchipped and details of its vaccinations will be entered in the passport. In the UK you can obtain a passport from a vet authorised to issue them. You can also download a passport form, and obtain up-to-date information (including details of the latest transport companies authorised to carry pets) from the website of the Department for Environment Food and Rural Affairs (DEFRA), www.defra.gov.uk. Defra also runs a Pets Helpline 0845 933 5577.

Cats and dogs under three months old can be taken to France before they are vaccinated. They still need a passport, and you will be required to certify that your pet has remained at the same location since it was born and either that it has had no contact with wild animals that are likely to have been exposed to rabies, or that it is still dependent on its mother and is accompanied by her. You must travel with your pet or meet it at the port of entry.

Taking your pet on the reverse journey is more complicated. UK regulations provide that your pet must also have a blood test to verify that the vaccine has worked. You will have to wait at least one month after the vaccination before your pet can have the blood test. After that your pet must wait for a further six months before it is allowed into the UK. It is best to leave about eight months in all. Your dog or cat must undergo treatment for ticks and tapeworm 24-48 hours before entering the UK. Under transitional arrangements pets issued with UK PETS certificates issued up until 30.09.04 may enter both the UK and France.

It is advisable to vaccinate dogs in France against hepatitis, parvovirus, leptospirosis, distemper, and kennel cough and to ensure that they receive an annual rabies booster. The disease leishmaniasis, generally only present in tropical and sub-tropical climates and transmitted by sandflies, is increasingly showing its face on the Côte d'Azur. Dogs are particularly vulnerable. There is no completely effective treatment once a dog has contracted the disease, nor is there a vaccination. The only course of action to counter it is to give your dog flea treatment to keep away the sandfly, though it is advisable to ask your vet to recommend a particular brand.

All dogs born after 06.01.99 must have either a tattoo in their ear, or a microchip inserted beneath the skin (usually in their neck). No anaesthetic is required for the insertion of a microchip which can be inserted painlessly, though a tattoo is put on under anaesthetic. Always attach a name tag with your address and telephone number to its collar.

Cats should be vaccinated against feline leukaemia and feline enteritis.

Pet health insurance costs around 160 euros per year for accidents and illnesses, and around 80 euros if cover is limited to accidents.

For details of kennels see the website www.royalcanin.fr (0800 415161), and for general information (in English) see www.dogsaway.co.uk.

Dogs and the heat

A dog should never, of course, be shut in a car – even with the windows open. You should endeavour to take your dog for a walk in the early morning or evening, and avoid exhausting it by playing ball or other strenuous exercise in the heat of the day. Some breeds cope very poorly with the heat and you may even need to spray your dog with water in addition to ensuring a steady supply of water to drink.

Dog-sitters

There is a network of dog-sitters on the Côte d'Azur, often retired people, who will look after your dog whilst you go away on holiday or for business, thereby avoiding the trauma of placing your canine friend and companion in a kennel. For example, www.dogsitting.asso.fr puts pet owners in touch with those willing to look after animals. There are currently around 250 members registered with the site in the Alpes-Maritimes, around 60% of these being dog-sitters. Dog-sitters charge between 10 and 15 euros a day depending on the size of your dog, and whether they have to feed it.

Other pets

At the time of writing there were no rules governing the import of guinea pigs, hamsters, rats, mice and gerbils entering either France or the UK. The import/export of animals such as birds, tropical fish and reptiles are subject to regulated control.

Lost and found

Lost or found pets should be reported (01 49 37 54 54 for dogs, and 01 55 01 08 08 for cats). If you lose your pet you should check whether it has been found and taken to the local pound (*fourrière*). The local *marie* will be able to provide you with the contact details. You may also derive assistance from the local branch of the SPA, (Société Protectrice des Animaux, www.spa.asso.fr) and information on stray animals at www.sanscollierprovence.org.

Animal refuges

There is an animal refuge at Eze (04 93 41 03 62) run by the SPA at Monaco, and another at Mougins. There is a cat refuge run by the Association Les Chats de Stella, 1460 ancien chemin de la Gaude, 06140 Vence.

CARS AND DRIVING

Importing and registering your car

You can import your car into France from the UK or Ireland without paying any additional VAT unless it is less than six months old. You will need to register your car within three months of arriving. To do this you must obtain a *certificat* from the local *Inspecteur des Mines*. The details of the address, etc. are available from the *Préfecture de Nice* (04 93 72 29 99) or the *Sous-Préfecture de Grasse*. Your vehicle must comply with French safety specifications – this will mean having the headlights modified. Once you have the *certificat* you should take this together with your passport, UK car registration documents, insurance certificate and any MOT certificate to the *Préfecture de Nice* (the St. Augustin exit on the A8) or the *Sous-Préfecture de Grasse (avenue Général de Gaulle)*. You will then be issued with a *Carte Grise* which will enable you to have your French registration plates fitted. There is a shop within a short distance from the *Sous-Préfecture de Grasse* where you should be able to have this done straightaway.

Driving licences

Any EU driving licence is sufficient to entitle you to drive on

French roads, although you must be aged over 18. Your non-French licence will not show your French address, which can cause problems if you are stopped by the police. The answer is to obtain an *Enregistrement d'un permis de conduire de l'Union Européene* (also called an F.45) from the *Préfecture*. This will record your French address and can then be stapled to your UK licence. There is no charge made for this. In practice many British and Irish residents on the Côte d'Azur do not bother obtaining an F.45. I have certainly never felt the need for an additional visit to queue at the *Préfecture*.

Drivers from non-EU countries will need to obtain a French licence. Australians, and citizens of some US states are entitled to exchange their licence for a French licence providing this is done within twelve months of the issue of their *carte de séjour*.

A UK or Ireland driving licence will cease to be valid in France if you commit a driving offence and receive penalty points – you must then obtain a French licence. Similarly, if are nearing 70 and your UK licence is about to expire you must apply for a French licence, and should do so several weeks before the expiry date of your UK licence.

Driving offences

Over the last two years the French authorities have, at last, begun to take drink-driving seriously. The limit is 0.5 g per litre of blood and offenders receive six penalty points (the maximum before you lose your licence is 12). You will automatically lose your licence if you commit a second offence with more than 0.8 g of alcohol in your blood, and you will receive a fine of up to 9,000 euros.

The police are likewise clamping down on speeding – one point if you are over 20 km per hour above the limit, four points for speeds of 40–50 km per hour over the limit and six points for speeds above that. Fixed and mobile radar traps have now been introduced right across the country.

Car insurance

Car insurance costs have started to fall as a result of the reduction in the number of accidents which has followed the clamp down on drink-driving and speeding.

MAAF (0820 300 820; www.maaf.fr) is quite competitive, though as always it pays to obtain several quotes, including from the local English-speaking insurers, Riviera Insurance Brokers (rue de la Paroisse 06560 Valbonne, 04 93 12 36 11). Always carry a *Constat Amiable* in the vehicle. You will need to fill this in and send it to your insurers in the event of an accident. Care is required in filling this out. The document is signed by both parties, and it is extremely difficult to go back on anything contained in it at a later date. You can obtain copies of this in English.

Contrôle Technique

A car must pass a *Contrôle Technique* in the six months prior to the end of its fourth year. This 133-point test costs around 60 euros and must be carried out every two years thereafter. Addresses of local centres can be found in the Yellow Pages under *Contrôle Technique* where there is also a helpful section explaining what is involved. You must carry out any work identified as necessary by the *contrôle* within two months. If you fail to do this, your car must undergo a complete retest.

OPENING AND RUNNING A BANK ACCOUNT

Account holders are provided with a cheque book and *carte bleue* that can be used as a payment card supported by your PIN and also for making withdrawals from cash machines. There is no point in post-dating a cheque as it can be drawn on immediately. You will be asked to produce ID whenever you issue a cheque. Banks impose limits on how much cash you can withdraw in any one month and will apply this even if you have plenty of funds in your account. You should ask your bank to increase the monthly amount you can take out if you think that your present limit may cause problems.

Loss or suspected theft of a cheque book or card should be reported immediately to your bank. Prompt reporting should limit your liability to €150. If you lose several cards you will have to contact each issuer separately, unless you take out a policy with Card Protection Plus, which can cover both your French and British cards (www.cpp.co.uk). There is currently no French equivalent.

Cheques remain valid for one year and eight days. If you are resident in France the law states that you must pay by cheque or card, but not cash, for purchases above 3,000 euros. You may usually only stop a cheque (*faire opposition*) if it has been lost or stolen. You should either contact your branch or telephone 0892 68 32 08. You must confirm your instructions in writing.

Bank charges

Bank charges in France are high, and in response to government pressure, the banks have recently taken measures to make their charges more transparent. You can find details of the banks that are currently the most competitive on the website www.testepourvous.com. La Poste is one of the cheapest.

If you have a complaint about your bank's services you should first raise this with the branch manager. Thereafter, if you are not satisfied with their response you should write to the bank's *médiateur.*

Overdrafts

Avoid letting your account become overdrawn or exceeding an overdraft limit *(le découvert)*. If you think that there is a risk that this might happen, telephone the person in charge of your account and explain the situation. If you issue a cheque *sans provision* (i.e. without funds in your account) it will be returned to the payee. If the payee does not receive payment within 30 days they can request a *certificat de non paiement* which they send to the payer by letter *avec accusé de réception*. They may then instruct a *huissier* to contact the issuer. The *huissier* can arrange for the sum to be deducted from the issuer's salary, together with various costs incurred. They can even arrange for goods to be seized and sold.

At the same time the issuer's bank accounts are frozen pending the payment to the payee of the cheque. There are significant financial penalties involved in issuing a cheque without the funds to cover it – a third of the value of each cheque over 50 euros! If the fines are not paid you could be subject to an *interdiction bancaire* for up to five years when you will have only limited access to banking facilities.

Relevé d'identité bancaire (RIB)

At the back of your cheque book you will find several detachable slips called a *RIB* or *relevé d'identité bancaire.* You can use these where you need to make regular payments to the same payee. Alternatively utility bills have a detachable slip with the identical details and if you sign and return this, the payee can similarly have sums deducted from your bank account.

Transferring money to France

This can, of course, be arranged over the telephone. Your bank may tell you that a transfer may take up to five working days to be credited to your French account, though often the funds are available the same or the next working day. Ensure that your bank applies the commercial rate for converting sterling into euros as it is significantly higher than the tourist rate: you may need to ask them how much money you need to transfer in order to benefit from preferential rates.

Your French bank may not make a charge for receiving sums in euros if you can quote your 27-digit IBAN in full (this is an international bank identification number which your French bank will supply you with), though the bank sending the funds may levy a fixed fee of £20–30 per transfer, irrespective of the amount. If your banks are part of the same group the charge may be lower.

The EU Savings Tax Directive

This has been introduced to ensure that those with offshore bank accounts comply with their obligations to pay tax on their *world-wide* income. It applies across Europe to interest earned on bank deposits, interest from certain bonds, and income from certain types of investment funds. Banks are obliged to levy a withholding tax on their account holders, or to supply details of interest received to the tax authorities in the account holder's country of residence. The banks will ask account holders to decide which options to select. The withholding tax is presently set at 15% but will rise to 20% in July 2008 and to 35% by 2011.

HOME INSURANCE

Home and public liability insurance are compulsory in France. The vast majority of comprehensive policies (*assurances multirisques habitation*) include public liability. You should inform your insurer or insurance broker if you are going to be away from your home for a long period or if you let it out. You may well be charged an increased premium, but if you do not inform them you may not be entitled to claim on your policy. If you do need to make a claim, do so immediately. Policies usually require policy holders to report thefts and break-ins to the police within 24 hours and to notify them of a claim within only a few days. A failure to do either may permit them to avoid meeting a claim.

In France a contract of insurance is automatically renewed. This has the disadvantage that if you wish to change insurers you must plan ahead and give your insurers adequate notice that you do not wish to renew. On the other hand, it has the major advantage that if you forget to pay the annual premium on time you will still be covered.

UK STATE BENEFITS

You are entitled to receive benefits such as invalidity and disability benefits, widows' benefits or benefits received as a result of an accident at work, or an occupational disease, wherever you live.

The payments should be made gross. Those living within the EU will also benefit from increases in the level of payment. Incapacity benefit is only paid to those who have paid Class 1 or Class 2 and 4 National Insurance contributions.

If you live in France, but are still paying UK income tax and National Insurance contributions you or your spouse remain entitled to non-means tested UK child benefit.

Ask the Department for Work and Pensions (International Services) at Longbenton, Newcastle-Upon-Tyne NE98 1YX. (0191 225 4811; www.dwp.gov.uk) to send you leaflet SA29 'Your Social Security, Insurance, Benefits and Health Care Rights in the European Community'. You should also obtain the leaflet entitled 'Social Security for Migrant Workers' available from the Department for Work and Pensions, Pensions and Overseas Benefits Directorate, Tyneview Park, Whitley Road, Benton, Newcastle-upon-Tyne NE98 1BA. (0191 2187777).

FRENCH STATE BENEFITS

Providing that you are working and paying tax and social security contributions in France, you are eligible to apply for state benefits in France on the same basis as a French citizen. National Insurance contributions that you have paid in the UK will be taken into account in determining your entitlement. Unemployment benefit is fixed at 75% of the minimum wage, currently around 340 euros per month. Income support is referred to as the *RMI, le revenu minimum d'intervention.*

YOUR *RÉGIME MATRIMONIAL*

In France married couples have the choice of several different *régimes* that will govern the financial relationship between them, and with other people. Under the option *le communauté des biens* all the assets acquired by husband and wife during their marriage belong to them both. This includes assets in the sole name of each. *Le régime séparation des biens* resembles the law in the UK with each spouse owning all assets individually, except those that they specifically decide to own jointly, such as their home or a joint bank account. Most British and Irish couples prefer to retain a separate system of general ownership, especially if one of them is in business. The choice of *régime* can have important tax and inheritance implications, and it is advisable to take advice from a lawyer or accountant.

PACTE CIVIL DE SOLIDARITE (PACS)

This relatively recent option permits two adults living together, including adults of the same sex, to formalise their relationship without entering into marriage. Those entering into a *PACS* gain certain rights (taxation, social security, housing, inheritance). Application for a *PACS* is made to the local *Tribunal d'Instance* (listed under *Tribunaux* in the Yellow Pages). There are various terms that can be included in a *PACS* and it is advisable to seek advice from an *avocat* or *notaire*. Fees range from 400 to 1,500 euros.

LA PROTECTION JURIDIQUE

I cannot emphasise strongly enough the importance of taking out such a policy. For an annual premium of less than £50 a year you usually have instant access to a telephone helpline for advice on most legal issues from problems with a noisy neighbour, to nuisance telephone calls or consumer problems. Policies cover you for defending a claim brought against you, or to bring a claim yourself. A legal-expenses policy can give you peace of mind, knowing that if you are involved in legal proceedings you will have most of your costs paid by your insurer. Policies do differ in the extent and type of cover, so you will need to check the main terms to see what is being offered.

HELP WITH THE AUTHORITIES

Les Centres Interministeriels de Renseignments Administratifs (CIRA) provide a single source of information or redirection for all questions from the public concerning work, tax, the courts, accommodation, social security, health, education, import duties, etc. (0821 08 09 10) This costs 0.12 euros per minute. See also www.service-public.fr.

ENERGY AUDIT

You can obtain an overall assessment of your energy needs and how to meet them by requesting a house inspection and report from ADEME – Agence de l'Environnement et la Maîtrise de l'Energie (0800 310 3111; www.ademe.fr). The cost is around 300 euros. The agency will also advise you about pollution and the grants and subsidies that you can obtain for using renewable fuels.

SOLAR ENERGY

The Côte d'Azur has more sun than anywhere else in France, and a significant number of homeowners in the area have installed solar systems to provide most of the energy they require for heating space and water. Solar systems are extremely economical, and will generally last for over twenty years. One drawback of a solar system is that even on the Côte d'Azur it is unlikely to provide you with all your hot water and heating every day of the year, and accordingly you will need a second source. Many people with solar systems have convenient and relatively cost-effective electric back-up hot water and heating systems.

The installation costs are high. A comprehensive system (*système solaire combiné*) for heating both space and water will set you back between 13,000 and 22,000 euros. If you opt for a hot-water only system (*chauffe eau-solaire individuel* or *CESI*) the outlay is reduced to just over a quarter of that cost.

There are grants and subsidies available from local and regional authorities. To benefit from these you must employ a certified installer (*agréé qualisol*) who can also provide you with up-to-date information on the funding available, the systems that attract funding and details of hire-purchase schemes. Details of certified *Qualisol* installers can be found on the ADEME website (*Base des Entreprises Qualisol*), and also in the Yellow Pages under *Energies solaires*. If you are a French taxpayer you will benefit from generous tax credits that cover up to 40% of the cost of solar heating for a principal residence.

AIR CONDITIONING

You may wish to include this on your list of essentials if you are looking for a property to buy or rent, and it is certainly worth obtaining an estimate for installing a system if you are buying your own property. In the south of France older people generally find that they need some means of lowering the temperature during the hot summer. Where a property has no central air conditioning, a convenient and reasonably economic alternative is to purchase a portable unit, though it's worth noting that some of the cheaper units can be very noisy.

ELECTRICITY

You will need to decide on the level of power supply you require and the type of tariff most suited to your needs. A small flat may only require a supply of 3.3 kWh, but for a family home you will probably need a supply of between 9 and 18kWh. If it is likely that several electrical appliances will be operating at the same time you could ask for a representative of EDF (Electricité de France) to advise on whether 18 kWh is sufficient – you may need to have a supply of up to 36kWh. This will be necessary if you wish to have the option of running a water-heating system, cooker, washing machine, dishwasher and other electrical consumer items simultaneously.

There are three different tariffs:

- The *option base* is a flat rate.

- The *option heures creuses* involves a higher subscription charge than the *option base* and enables you to take advantage of an off-peak tariff (about two thirds of the standard tariff) for eight hours a day usually between 01.00 to 07.30 and 12.30 to 02.00 EDF may agree to you adjusting these times.

* The *tempo tarif* is particularly suited for holiday homes. This has a much lower rate per kWh throughout most of the year. The downside is that you pay a significantly higher rate for 43 days of the year (*jours blancs*) and a very much higher rate on 22 high peak days (*jours rouges*) between November and March. These dates are published in advance by EDF. Ask your EDF adviser about installing a warning system to alert you to when a change in the tariff is imminent.

Power cuts and surges

We have experienced a significant number of power cuts during our years on the Côte d'Azur, as well as several power surges during storms. The latter can seriously damage electrical appliances such as modems. You may wish to consider buying a UPS (uninterruptable power supply, which costs around 150 euros). A surge protector (costing around 18 euros) is also a worthwhile investment, certainly for the protection of your computer.

EMERGENCIES

Should you need to contact EDF/GDF the emergency number is on the top left of your electricity bill. Alternatively telephone 0810 12 61 26 for EDF and 0810 14 01 59 for GDF (Gaz de France). They promise to attend within four hours of a call, and immediately in the case of a suspected gas leak.

You can find further information about EDF and GDF, including their tariffs, on their websites ww.edf.fr and www.gazdefrance.fr.

Both organisations publish leaflets in English setting out their services and charges.

WATER

All mains water supplies are metered. The consumption of an average family can easily reach 500 litres of water per day. This can be significantly reduced by taking showers and installing modern toilet cisterns. Dripping taps can also be expensive and could easily add 25% or more to a household's consumption. You can find out if your system has leaks by taking a reading last thing at night, and another first thing in the morning before using your water supply. You should check in any event where your meter is. In some cases meters are often some distance from your property, perhaps up the hill, and you would never guess that the meter related to your property rather than another house! You should also ascertain the location of the main stop-valve or stopcock so that you can turn off the water supply in an emergency.

THE TELEPHONE

You can find detailed information about telephone services on France Telecom's website www.francetelecom.com. You can arrange a connection by telephoning 1014. If you do not wish your number to be included in the telephone directory, ask to be included in the *liste rouge*. You can stop your details being added to publicity mailing lists by requesting your details be added to the *liste orange*.

Special telephone numbers

For telephone enquiries telephone 118 218. *Numeros verts* (prefixes 0800, 0805, 0809, 0819) are free from a land line or telephone boxes, with normal national rates applying from mobile telephones. *Numeros azur* (0810, 0811) are charged at local rates from a land line, with charges from mobile telephones varying between operators. *Numeros indigos* (0820, 0821) are charged at 0.12 euros a minute with a minimum charge of one minute. Rates from mobile telephones vary according to the operator. Audiotel numbers (0890, 0891, 0892): charges depend on the particular service, but start at 0.15 euros a minute and can be as high as 1.20 euros per minute.

Special services

You can find out the number of the last person who rang you by dialling 3131. You can withhold your own number by dialling 3651 before dialling the number required. As you would expect, France Telecom has all the standard telephone services such as call transfer (*Le Transfert d'Appel),* and also an enquiry service in English 0800 364 775. You can also find information on telephone services in the front pages of the Yellow Pages and at www.francetelecom.com/en/tools/others/contactus.html.

Holiday home telephones

If you have a holiday home and wish to temporarily suspend your telephone line when you are not there ask for details of *la Ligne Résidence Secondaire.* Another service is *Téléséjour* which enables you to keep your line active to receive calls, but limits outgoing calls to emergency and free numbers.

UTILITY BILLS FOR THE HANDICAPPED OR THOSE IN RECEIPT OF *RMI*

Those in receipt of supplementary benefit (*RMI* or *Revenu Minimum d'Insertion*) or who have a recognised handicap, are entitled to reduced rates for electricity, water and telephone. You can obtain details of the scheme from your *mairie*.

MOBILE TELEPHONES

The main operators are SFR, Bouygues Telecom and Orange. You can now change provider without changing your number. If your telephone is stolen, you must notify the police and your service supplier immediately (Orange 08 25 00 57 00; Bouygues 08 00 29 10 00; and SFR 06 10 00 19 00). You will be asked for your mobile phone identification code and accordingly you should ensure that you have a note of this (it is usually beside or behind the battery). It is advisable to have insurance for your mobile telephone especially to cover telephone calls made after it is stolen if you do not have a limit on the calls that can be made.

Mobile telephone operators are now required to notify you within one to three months before the renewal date. The contract is automatically renewed if you do nothing.

THE POSTAL SERVICE

Letters are generally delivered the next day within France. Letters to and from the UK can take only two days, but often take three or four working days. Post can be redirected for up to six months. Ask for a *Contrat de Réexpédition ou de Garde du Courrier* at your local post office. Post offices are open from 08.00 to 18.00 in the week and also on a Saturday morning but are usually closed for lunch. Most branches have Fax and Minitel services. You can avoid the queues by using the automated service for weighing and paying for letters and parcels, and by purchasing stamps at a *tabac*.

Mail at an empty house

It is never a good idea to advertise your absence by allowing mail to stack up whilst you are away causing letters to protrude out of your letter box. The are various options to avoid this. You could have your post redirected to your holiday address at a cost of under 20 euros, or a little more for a destination in another EU country. A slightly cheaper alternative is to have your post held for you at your local post office (*garde du courrier*).

TELEVISION AND SATELLITE RECEIVERS

If you have a television in your home you are liable to pay the television licence fee irrespective of whether or not you watch French television. The fee is payable per household, irrespective of the number of television sets in the house. If you buy a television set in France the seller is required by law to inform the authorities and supply them with your details. You should automatically receive a request for payment. The licence fee (*redevance télé*) is now collected with the *taxe d'habitation*. Those aged 65 and over who were not liable to pay any income tax for the previous year are exempt, as are those earning less than about 7,200 euros who have a disability of 80% or more. Analogue French television is available via a standard aerial, digital television is available via an aerial in some regions, or via satellite throughout France.

You can receive UK television by installing a satellite receiver. BBC 1, BBC 2, ITV, Channel 4, Channel 5 and Sky can be obtained by purchasing a receiver from specialists and a card from the UK. This is illegal and in breach of licence and copyright laws which limit the card's use to within the UK, though in practice many people do this. You can also obtain British TV through your broadband connection in some regions and via some internet service providers.

INTERNET

There is a range of service providers. ADSL is less expensive on the whole than it is in the UK. You can compare different operators' ADSL prices in France by visiting www.ariase.com/fr/observatoire/fai/adsl.html (for dial-up rates see www.ariase.com/fr/observatoire/fai/56.html). Much of the Alpes-Maritimes has ADSL coverage. To find out whether a commune has ADSL see www.degrouptest.com. France Telecom is currently putting considerable effort into extending its lines in the Var and claims that 98.9% of homes in the department will have access to ADSL by the end of 2006.

MEETING FRENCH PEOPLE

An easy way of meeting local people is by participating in the numerous cultural, sporting and social associations that can be found in most French towns, or by joining one of the evening classes run by the local *mairie,* or the local branch of the AVF (see Chapter 1 for more information about this association). Certainly becoming involved in the AVF itself will enable you to quickly make friends and acquaintances. Parents with children at school often have opportunities through the school and through their children of meeting French people. The French are generally slower than Anglo-Saxons at 'breaking the ice' and you may need to discretely take the initiative. You should try not to call on your French friends and neighbours without an invitation or at least a warning.

FRENCH – ACQUIRING THE LANGUAGE

French is a difficult language, even for the French. School children in France certainly spend considerable time mastering their language. However, if you are serious about integrating into France or wish to confidently handle day-to-day relations with French people and deal with emergency situations, you need to be able to speak and to understand French with ease.

In the UK

It is a good idea to begin studying the language before moving to France. There are, of course, many night classes in French up and down the UK. Those living in London or Manchester should take advantage of the courses run by the French Institute. The *Alliance Francaise* runs courses in Bath, Belfast, Bristol, Cambridge, Exeter, Glasgow, Jersey, Milton Keynes and York as well as London and Manchester.

In France

Once on the Côte d'Azur you will find that many local councils and branches of the AVF arrange French classes, all of which are inexpensive. The ANPE holds free classes in French for the unemployed. In addition there are several private organisations that run courses (see for example in The French Directory: Learn in France at www.europa-pages.com). You can study for GCSE and A level through the National Extension College. It is also possible to study with the Open University which has a diploma in French and a degree in Modern Language Studies. (For further information on the OU, see Chapter 5.) Another option is an External Degree in French Studies at London University. Alternatively you could study for one of the examinations to determine your level of French held by the French authorities, such as the *Diplôme d'Etude de la Langue Française*.

The expression 'use it or lose it' applies as much to the acquisition of French as it does to retaining your knowledge. Converse in French as much as you can. The most effective way is also the most economic: make French friends. The second most effective means, also inexpensive, is to watch French television, especially those programmes that are the easiest to follow such as children's cartoons. News presenters are amongst the clearest speakers. Translations of American and British films are usually far easier to follow than French films which tend to contain more colloquial terms.

GOOD AND BAD NEIGHBOURS

The French are much more formal than Anglo-Saxons or Celts. The Australian soap *Neighbours* lasted only a very short time on French television before it was withdrawn: the content was just too foreign and unfamiliar to French viewers. It is nevertheless a good idea to introduce yourself to your neighbours, and try to establish a good rapport at an early stage. If you live in a flat you could take advantage of the annual event *Les Immeubles en Fête* in which an estimated 2 million residents in urban areas take part and attempt to get to know each other.

If you do have a disagreement with a neighbour (and neighbour disputes are a frequent subject of documentaries on French television) you should seek to reach agreement between yourselves, or perhaps ask a neutral third party to act as a conciliator or arbitrator. Legal proceedings in neighbour disputes invariably share three characteristics, they are: expensive, stressful and disappointing. If you have a legal expenses insurance policy, this may reduce the expense of bringing or defending a claim. You can find out how to contact an absent neighbour by asking at the local *mairie*.

As to noise levels, pollution and other nuisances you are generally obliged to put up with nuisances that have been present in your locality for years, such as the ringing of church bells on a Sunday morning. There is a legal noise limit of 30 dB (decibels) above the normal background noise. Noises in excess of this limit are punishable with a fine of up to 450 euros. Information on excessive noise levels can be obtained at www.bruit.fr. Initial advice in relation to disagreements, generally with neighbours, is available from the Association de Défense des Victimes de Troubles du Voisinage, 8, allée de la Forêt 78170 La Celle-Saint-Cloud. (01 39 69 26 88; www.nuisances.advtv.free.fr/)

CUTTING BACK TREES AND VEGETATION

Recent summers have seen extensive forest fires in the Var. The law now requires property owners and occupiers to cut back trees and vegetation (*le débroussaillement*) within a radius of 50 metres of property. There are further regulations, details of which are available at www.ofme.org; www.debrouissaillement.com.

CONSUMER PROTECTION

Advice is available from La Commission de la Sécurité des Consommateurs (CSC); www.securiteconso.org. There is an English translation of much of the website. The advice line covers all administrative and consumer enquiries (Tel: 39 39) and is open 08.00 to 19.00 Mon to Fri and 09.00 to 14.00 on Saturdays. It costs €0.12 per minute. If you feel that you have been the victim of a fraud or fraudulent transaction you should contact *Direction Générale de la Concurrence de la Consommation et de la Repression des Fraudes*(*DGCCRF*) (0800 20 22 03).

TRADE ESTIMATES

The law requires tradespeople to provide quotations *(les devis)* for work costing in excess of €150, setting out the work to be undertaken and the price. Unless your agreement with the tradesperson entitles them to charge more than quoted, they are limited to the price quoted. If the tradesperson refuses to honour his quotation you should obtain further advice from the *Direction Départementale de la Concurrence de la Consommation et de la Repression des Fraudes* (*DDCCRF*).

THE BLACK MARKET

Do not be tempted to use traders who are working illegally. Insist on proof that they are properly registered with the social security authorities and have professional insurance. Ask to see their *carte d'identification* issued by the *Chambre de Métiers*. There are a significant number of Britons working illegally on the Côte d'Azur. If you do have work carried out by these people and one of them were to have an accident, they may well seek to argue that they were employed by you, and that accordingly you should pay the costs of medical treatment. Should they cause damage to your property but are uninsured, you may not be able to recover the cost of putting matters right. You can obtain details of tradespeople who can speak English on www.artisan-anglais.com which provides a registration number for each business.

EMPLOYING PEOPLE IN YOUR HOME

There are different *Conventions Collectives* that govern the obligations of employers of gardeners, childminders or other staff, including pay, accommodation, dismissal, etc. These may require employers to give three months' notice of termination of employment and this probably applies also to the vacation of any accommodation provided by the employer.

If you employ anyone in your home, including on a part-time, temporary or even irregular basis, such as a cleaner, gardener or babysitter, you must notify the authorities and pay social security contributions. If you fail to do so you can face significant fines.

The system of *Le Chèque Emploi Service* was specifically introduced for those employing people in their homes (see Chapter 3).

MOVING HOUSE

There is now a website where you can notify a change of address to be passed on to all other government agencies (www.changement-adresse.gouv.fr), such as the CAF, CPAM, and Assedic.

VOTING

Resident UK and other citizens of EU member states have the right to vote and stand in French municipal or European elections. Applications to be listed on the electoral register are made to your local *mairie*.

There are several British citizens who have been elected to posts including Sue Dunnachie in Mougins, and Tracey Glowinski in Bar-sur-Loup.

MANAGING DISABILITIES

Wheelchair users in the region can contact S. Odgers, odger1@yahoo.com for information about facilities in the region. The most accessible beach for wheelchair users is definitely the Handiplage at St. Laurent-du-Var. Parc Phoenix, the Nice tropical floral garden, and Galeries La Fayette also in Nice are both user-friendly for those in wheelchairs. Whilst the SNCF is legally required to improve wheelchair access to train stations, the company has a long way to go. The main stations in Nice and Monaco are no exceptions.

For information for handicapped persons contact COTOREP (Commission Technique d'Orientation et de Reclassement

Professionel) which has an office in Nice (04 93 72 65 00), and for the range of financial assistance available contact the local CPAM, Caisse Primaire d'Assurance Maladie.

INSECT STINGS

The French Riviera is host to a wide variety of wasps, mosquitoes and scorpions. Indeed France has fifty different species of mosquito. Whilst none of those native to France are carriers of disease, in the hot season, foreign mosquitoes can trespass into the country, and they can be more dangerous. Children especially should be cautioned to avoid hives and nests, and not to walk barefoot in country areas. You should also ensure that you do not wear brightly-coloured clothes, or strong perfume that is likely to attract insects. If planning a picnic, take a tablecloth with you that has been impregnated with a repellent, and always carry a tube of cream that is effective against allergies. Some people apply citronella or garlic to their skin, others place slices of tomatoes or oranges on their bodies to deter insects: there are also many proprietary insect repellents available in chemists (*pharmacies*).

HOME SECURITY

There are a number of measures that you can take to secure your premises against intruders. Installing an alarm system and a PVC rolling shutter system are two steps worth considering. Some shutters respond to movement and if touched whilst closed sound an alarm. Another variant is a system with a hand-held remote control, not just for opening and closing the shutters, but also for setting of the alarm. A cheap but simple and effective deterrent is to purchase a timer switch (costing around 25 euros or less) that will switch your lights and/or radio or television on and off at set times when you are away from the house.

A number of companies provide a 24-hour tele-surveillance system such as Azur Security (04 93 12 18 79; info@azursecurity.com), and promise to intervene speedily if a problem arises. iDomus (www.idomus.uk.com), a UK based company, supplies systems with internal and external day and night cameras together with digital image recorders that transmit information to the company's monitoring centre. Even more sophisticated systems enable you to set the alarm, control your central heating, or view around your property wherever you are. These systems can cost up to €15,000 depending upon the equipment required. A simple system involving four radio transmitted noise detectors, an alarm system and a remote control would cost a little over €1,000.

One option that needs to be exercised with care is to have a house sitter. The site www.ani-seniors.fr will put you in contact with retired people prepared to look after your home and garden in return for a stay in your Riviera home.

LOST PROPERTY

If you lose an item in Nice or the Alpes-Maritimes do not assume that all is lost. Thousands of items each year, many of value, are handed in by members of the public and find their way to the Service des Objets Trouvés on rue Raoul Bosio in Nice. If you find an item, obtain a receipt. Generally a finder becomes entitled to property that is not claimed within a year and a day of being handed in. Should you lose an item of value, or a set of car keys, in the sand, or in your garden, consider turning to L'Association Française des prospecteurs (01 43 07 55 99). This is a free service staffed by enthusiastic volunteers armed with metal detectors.

TAKING FRENCH NATIONALITY

Should you wish to take on French nationality you must be over 18 and have resided in France for at least five years. This is reduced to two years for those who have already completed at least two years of further education in France. To be eligible you must also be able to speak and write French to a 'reasononable' standard, not have any criminal conviction punishable with a sentence of six months or more of imprisonment and demonstrate loyalty to France. You must also derive your earnings from France.

Applications for citizenship are made to the *Préfecture* in Nice, and take around twelve months to process. Different rules apply to those who marry a French citizen and to children born in France.

8
Schools

PRE-SCHOOL EDUCATION

Many British and other foreign parents often opt for French pre-school education. It is generally free or heavily subsidised and enables young children to have early exposure to the French language at an age when they are most receptive to learning it. A number of parents keep their children in the French system during their primary education and only move them to an English or International school from age 12.

Pre-school education consists of *crèches* (day nurseries often run by the local authority for children from two months to three years) and *halte-garderies* (for children between three months and six years). Another option is to place your child with an *assistante maternelle* or registered childminder looking after one or more children in her home. It is advisable to book places in *crèches* and *halte-garderies* well in advance. Local *mairies* generally keep lists of registered childminders. Placing a child with an *assistante maternelle*, in a *crèche* or a *halte-garderie* entitles tax payers to a tax credit equal to 25% of the cost. If you opt to employ someone to look after your children in your own home (*une garde d'enfant*),

50% of the cost of the salary and social security costs associated with employing that person can be deducted from your income for tax purposes.

State nursery school is available from the age of around 4. Often part of a primary school, nursery schools are divided into three years:

* *la petite section*;

* *la moyenne section*;

* *la grande section*.

You will need proof of vaccinations for diphtheria, tetanus, poliomyelitis and tuberculosis as a condition of school entry.

PRIVATE FRENCH SCHOOLS

Many private French schools, including most of the Catholic schools are *sous-contrat* – this means that they are independent but that the salaries of their teaching staff are financed by the state. Their fees are accordingly lower than private schools in the UK. It is generally considered that Catholic schools provide a more protected environment and that educational standards are higher than in state schools. Private schools are listed in the *Pages Jaunes* under *Enseignement primaire: écoles privées* and *Enseignement secondaires: collèges privés*. You can find more information about French private schools from Le Centre Nationale de Documentation sur l'Enseignement Privé, 20, rue Faubert, 75007 Paris. (01 47 05 32 68 or see their website: www.fabert.com)

STATE SCHOOLS

Though attendance at state schools is free, the state requires parents to take responsibility for supplying exercise books and other school materials. Children generally have to attend their nearest school, and if the family moves house the child will usually be expected to change schools. Though this is subject to exceptions, some parents prefer to choose a private school to avoid this. To apply for state schools you should generally contact your local *mairie*.

Schools are, of course, mixed, with no uniform. Sport, drama and music have only a limited role in French schools – children are normally expected to pursue these activities outside of school.

There is more flexibility in France than in the UK as to the age at which a child starts primary school. Within each school year there is quite a range of ages. If a child is experiencing difficulties at school he or she may be asked to *redoubler* i.e. repeat the school year.

The school year starts in September, and finishes around the end of June. Normal school hours are 08.00 or 08.15 to 16.00 for primary schools and 16.30 for secondary schools. Lunchtime is generally around 11.30 with a two-hour break. French schools do not tend to have organised activities during the lunch break.

Each year, before school starts, parents receive a list of school materials to purchase, different types of exercise books and a range of items for a child's pencil case. The build up to *la rentrée* or start of term is so frenetic that it is regularly covered on national and local television with parents interviewed to recount how they are coping with this annual frenzy. The cost of all the material that is required is considerable. Indeed the government provides a means-tested grant of around 250 euros that is currently being paid to almost three million families. Details of how to claim can be obtained from your local *caisse d'allocations familiales.*

PRIMARY SCHOOL (*ÉCOLE PRIMAIRE*)
6 TO 11 YEARS

The primary years are divided into three cycles:

* Year 1: CP (*Cours Préparatoire*);

* Years 2 & 3: CE1 and CE2 (*Cours Elémentaires*);

* Years 4 & 5: CM1 and CM2 (*Cours Moyens*).

There are national tests at the beginning of CE2. Children are not given any preparation for these, though the result will be kept with the child's school records. The test is designed to identify those children with significant educational problems.

A considerable number of primary schools operate for only half a day on Wednesdays (finishing at around 11.15), whilst others have no school on Wednesdays at all, but have slightly longer school terms. Primary school teachers are known as *maître* or *maîtresse*.

SECONDARY SCHOOL (*COLLEGE*)
11 TO 16 YEARS

The first two terms of secondary school are intended to assess your child's ability and to ensure that they have mastered the main concepts taught during the primary school years. It is only in the summer term that students will begin to move on to new ground.

Collège is divided into three cycles:

* *sixième*: (1st year) – *observation et orientation*;

* *cinquième* & *quatrième*: (2nd & 3rd years) – *cycle central*;

* *troisième*: (4th year) – *orientation*.

A child can again be required to repeat the last year of each cycle. The objective of the last year of *collège* (i.e. *troisième*) is to decide a child's future educational path. At the end of *troisième* each child sits state examinations called *le brevet*.

Many parents from the UK have noticed a striking difference between how a child in the last year of primary school is treated and how a child one year older in the first year of secondary school is treated. From being treated like very young children, they are suddenly treated like adolescents, immediately given much more freedom.

The school day

One problem that parents have is managing the 'holes' in the secondary school day. Your child will normally start school at 08.00 but may have no classes from 11.00 to 15.00. Children are expected to undertake private study either in the library (*Le Centre de Documentation et d'Information – Le CDI*), or to attend a designated room where they remain under the surveillance of often a non-teaching member of staff. Parents from the UK are often not at all enthusiastic about this free time.

Hotel Negresco, Nice

La Fête des citrons, Menton

Promenade des Anglais, Nice

Old town, Nice

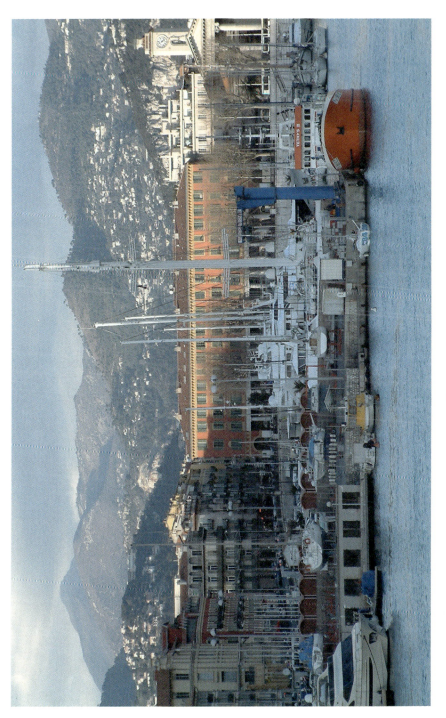

Old port, Nice

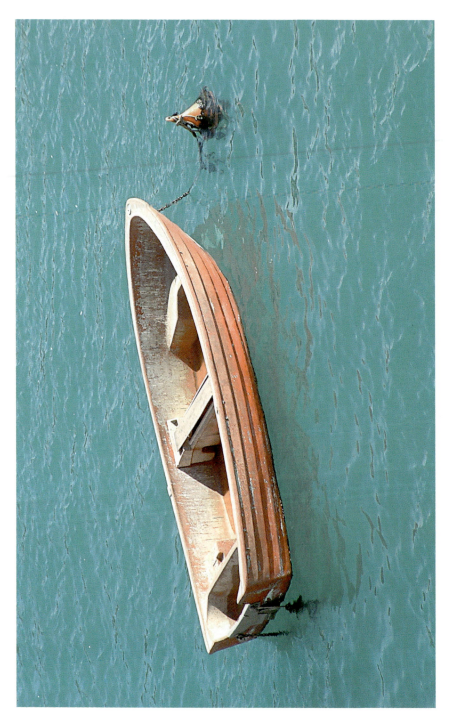

Villefranche sur Mer

Villefranche sur Mer

Villa Ephrussi de Rothschild, St Jean Cap Ferrat

Cannes

First year in secondary school

You can find information about your child's first year in *collège* by obtaining the guide *L'entrée en 6e – le guide des parents* published by the Office National d'Information sur les Enseignements et les Professions (ONISEP) which you can obtain at a cost of €3.50. This, and a variety of career guides can be obtained from ONISEP (www.onisep.fr; 01 64 80 38 00).

At the start of secondary school children take national tests (*évaluations*) in mathematics and French. Pupils are not prepared for these tests which are designed to identify children in difficulty who require extra help.

Conseil de Classe

Each class in the *collège* has a *Conseil de Classe* that meets at the end of each term. Those participating will include two elected representatives from among parents at the school and two elected representatives from the class (*les délégués de classe*). The *Conseil de Classe* discusses every child's progress during the term, and any problems that might be influencing their academic progress such as health, or family circumstances. The role of the *délégués de classe* is to represent the children before the *Conseil de Classe*.

Baccalauréat

After the *brevet* children move up to the *lycée* where they study for the *baccalauréat* or *le bac* from the age of around 16 to 18 (*deuxième*, *première* and *terminale*.) In addition to the science *bac*, literary *bac* and general *bac* there are more vocational *bacs*. All students studying for the non-vocational courses will study maths, French and a foreign language.

EQUIVALENT EDUCATIONAL YEAR GROUPS IN FRANCE AND THE UK

Age	UK school year	French school year
2–3	nursery	*Maternelle (Petite Section* and *Moyenne Section)*
5–6	1	*Maternelle (Grande Section)*

École Primaire

Age	UK school year	French school year
6–7	2	*CP*
7–8	3	*CE1*
8–9	4	*CE2*
9–10	5	*CM1*
10–11	6	*CM2*

Collège

Age	UK school year	French school year
11–12	7	*6ième*
12–13	8	*5ième*
13–14	9	*4ième*
14–15	10	*3ième*

Lycée

15–16	11	*2ième*
16–17	12	*Première*
17–18	13	*Terminale*

EDUCATING YOUR CHILD ON THE CÔTE D'AZUR

Education always involves difficult decisions for parents. This is true of the French Riviera, just as elsewhere. A school life spent in the south of France sounds privileged, and indeed in many ways it is. It is not without its problems, however.

LEARNING FRENCH

Many parents expect that after a few years schooling in France their child should have become almost fluent in the French language. Research shows that the ability of a child to learn a foreign language is at its greatest before the age of six, and that thereafter learning a foreign language becomes progressively more difficult. Whilst children can and do become fluent in French and English, this requires considerable exposure to both languages as well as determination and hard work from both child and parents. This is especially so for children who start their exposure to bilingualism after the age of six. In practice most English children who speak a high level of French have been to a French school and/or have a French parent.

PRIVATE INTERNATIONAL SCHOOLS

There are, of course, several private international schools on the Côte d'Azur. They are all good at marketing.

All the international schools claim to provide their students with a high level of education. It is notable, however, that their literature and websites seldom provide details of the qualifications of their teaching staff, or the academic results of their pupils. This is information that you might want to ask when you attend at interview.

It is worth remembering that these are international schools. They attract many foreign children from a wide range of countries whose parents choose an international school in large part because they want their child to learn to speak English to a high level. One can well understand these parents' motivation. Whilst in the UK a foreign language is not compulsory, for other Europeans English is now an essential element of their education and a vital tool for the ambitious student. Attendance at an international school is clearly a huge benefit for the child concerned, and it sounds good for international relations to have this mixture of nationalities. Not so good for your child, who may well be in a class where the majority of children, perhaps as many as two-thirds, are not native English speakers. Some of these children will speak English to a reasonable level, though a few will have only limited English at their disposal.

This mix of nationalities inevitably poses difficulties for teaching staff. Whilst your child may gain much from an education in an international environment, it is difficult to believe that the class in which he is in can study subjects such as English and History with the same maturity as they would if educated at a good school in the UK.

The private international schools tend to be fairly small. This has the advantage that teachers and pupils quickly get to know each other. A disadvantage is that they are inevitably limited in the curriculum that they can offer at GCSE and A-Level. You should also not assume that your child will be free to choose which subjects to take from those taught at the school. Timetabling will make some combinations impossible.

Another feature of these schools is the frequent turnover of pupils. Whilst undoubtedly some remain at the same school throughout their school career, many leave either for one of the other international schools in the area or more usually because their parents have to move for work reasons.

I have also been struck by the contrast between student life at the international schools and that back in the UK. The children are accorded considerably more freedom. This is particularly so at the Centre International de Valbonne (see below) where school life (from age 12), and the school campus, have more in common with a university than a school in the UK. This worries many parents.

ALTERNATIVES

In addition to French schools and private international schools there is another option. There are now a number of state schools in France, that have an Anglophone section. The Centre International de Valbonne is one such international school, which also has Italian and German sections. Again these schools are proud of their international status, and of being different. The creation and growth of such schools clearly provides parents with another choice in which their children can have a bilingual education at fees substantially less than the private international schools that are not delivering a bilingual education. Your child will not lose their English as some English children in French schools do.

PRIVATE INTERNATIONAL AND BILINGUAL SCHOOLS ON THE CÔTE D'AZUR

Mougins School

615, Avenue Dr. Maurice Donat, Font de L'Orme, BP 401, 06251 Mougins Cedex. (00 33 4 93 90 15 47; email information@moungins-school.com; website: www.mougins-school.com)

Mougins School has about 400 pupils from over thirty countries and takes children from nursery age to A-level. There is a shortage of places at primary school level where there is only one class per year, but from Year 7 there are two classes for each year and accordingly a greater availability of places. There is no entrance examination.

British curriculum

The school provides an education based on the British curriculum. The school states that it tests children according to the Key Stages, but marking is entirely internal. Besides French, they offer Spanish and German: in both cases tuition being given by native speakers. Sports are given considerable emphasis. Indeed the headteacher, Mr. Hickmore, is the head of sports at the school. The website states that the school has 'excellent' results at International GCSE and A-level. As yet details of examination results are not posted on the site or published in the school brochure.

Location

The school is located on a purpose-built site in the Sophia Antipolis business park. The wooden buildings are attractive, giving the campus almost the air of a holiday camp.

Social and domestic

There is an active parent-teacher association that organises social and fund-raising activities.

There is a school bus that picks up and drops off at stops between the school and Fréjus, including at the A8 junction at Mandelieu. The school day begins at 08.45 (three quarters of an hour later than French schools) and finishes at around 16.00. The school adopts the French practice of finishing at lunchtime on a Wednesday.

Fees

Fees currently range from around 9,000 euros in the first year of primary school to around 12,500 euros a year for older children. In addition there is a non-refundable application fee payable at the time of application of 600 euros for the first child, 450 euros for the second and 300 for the third. There is a 10% reduction if you have three children at the school and have no employer subsidy (presumably for the fees of all your children). You are required to give a term's notice if you wish your child to leave the school.

The International School of Nice

15, avenue Claude Debussy, Nice. (00 33 4 93 21 04 00; website: www.isn-nice.org)

This is a private international school owned by the French Riviera Chamber of Commerce and catering for children aged 4 to 18. It is less British than Mougins School and has more in common with European and American schools. It is accredited by the Middle States Association of the United States, as well as the European Council for International Schools. Its teaching staff are British, American and French and its pupils span over thirty different nationalities. Students take IGCSE but thereafter take the International Baccalaureate. According to its literature pupils stay for an average of six years, which is impressive amongst international schools, as they tend to have a rapid turnover of pupils for obvious reasons. In all there are around 300 pupils, though the school is adding a number of classes and is in the process of expanding.

Curriculum

Tuition is in English. The curriculum does not include any foreign languages, other than French. The headteacher, Dorothy Foster, told me that the school's priority was to achieve a high level of ability in French, and the school did not wish to jeopardise this by adding another foreign language. For many pupils this is clearly realistic, providing, that is, a high level of French is indeed attained. Class size is around 23.

Children over 10 whose native language is not English must take oral and written examinations in English, and a test in mathematics prior to admission.

Social and domestic

The site is to the west of Nice only five minutes from Nice Côte d'Azur airport. There are school buses that serve Tourettes sur Loup, Vence, St Paul, Cagnes-sur-Mer, Eze, Beaulieu, Villefranche, Valbonne, Mougins, Sophia Antipolis, Antibes, Cannes, Golf-Juan, Biot, Villeneuve Loubet, Monaco and Cap d'Ail.

There is an active parent-teacher association (for details contact valerie@madisononline.org).

The school day starts at 08.45 and goes on to 15.40. This applies to Wednesday as well as the other days of the week.

Fees

Annual school fees range from 9,000 to 12,500 euros depending on your child's age. There is an additional one-off admission payment of 950 euros. Should you wish your child to leave the school during the school year you will still be liable to pay the year's fees less a sliding rebate.

The International School of Monaco

12, quai Antoine 1er, MC 98000 Monaco. (00 377 93 25 68 20; email ecoleism@cote-dazur.com; website: www.ismonaco.org)

This is the most recent addition to the international schools on the

Riviera, having opened its doors in 1994, under the directorship of Scottish headteacher Mary Macaud. It takes children from three years old, through International GCSEs and up to the International Baccalaureate.

This mixed school has around 320 pupils, has small class sizes limited to 16, and claims to provide a bilingual international education. Around 25% of pupils are from the UK, 10% from US, 16% from Italy, and 11% from Germany. Spanish or Italian are offered as a third language, and in contrast to the other international schools mother tongue support is also given in these languages and also in German and Russian.

Fees

Annual tuition fees start at nearly 14,000 euros for Year 2, and rise to nearly 17,000 euros for the baccalaureate years. In addition there is a new student registration fee of 1,500 euros and a new student 'Capital Development Fee' of 3,500 euros. These are both non-refundable. The total fee package makes it the most expensive of the international schools, especially for those staying only for two or three years.

The International School of Sophia Antipolis

Rue du Vallon, Les Boullides, 06560 Sophia Antipolis.
(00 33 4 92 38 17 20; email admissions@civissa.org; website: www.issa.net)

This is a non profit-making international day and boarding-school situated in the Sophia Antipolis technology park. It is in close proximity to the CIV with which it has shared many facilities, though there has been substantial disagreement between the two institutions over the last couple of years. Mougins School is also not very far away.

Curriculum

The school covers the last four years of secondary school with the initial Foundation Programme leading to the International Baccalaureate. There are a total of about 150 students on these two programmes. The school places a strong emphasis on bilingualism.

The school describes its International Baccalaureate programme as 'highly academic'. Entrance is selective and candidates have to take entry tests in English, mathematics and French, followed by an interview which parents are also invited to attend. Those who are considering taking a bilingual diploma offered by the school are encouraged to take a different test in French, the same as that taken by native French applicants.

Fees

There is a fee of 350 euros payable on application to the school, and a registration fee of 1,500 euros if your child is accepted. School fees are currently around 10,000 euros for a day pupil.

École Privée Internationale Le pain d'épice

23, boulevard Gambetta 0600 Nice. (00 33 4 93 44 75 44; info@ecolepaindepice.com; website: www.ecoledupaindesucre.com)

École Privée Active Bilingue Le pain de sucre

43, chemin du pain de sucre, 08600 Cagnes-sur-Mer.
(00 33 4 93 73 70 41; email info@ecoledupaindesucre.com;
website: www.ecoledupaindesucre.com)

These two schools, each with nursery and primary sections, are very similar and both are under the auspices of the same headteacher, Madame Pascale Rosfelder-Alhadeff Both schools claim to offer a bilingual education with half the teaching in English and half in French. The modest websites of both schools have versions in English though if you download the brochure from the English pages of the site the brochure is in French. The site also serves the Collège Lafayette into which both primary schools feed. You can download that school's brochure from the website, but again, not in English.

School hours

Both primary schools are open from 7.30 in the morning until 18.30. Lessons in the primary school start at 8.30 and the school day finishes at 16.50. There is no formal school on a Wednesday, but the schools are open and provide a minding service. They are also open on a similar basis throughout most of the school holidays.

Curriculum

The schools ambitiously claim to follow the curriculum followed by English *and* American schools as well as that used in French schools and to use the same material. Class sizes are said to be between 15 and 20.

Fees

Though these are private schools and are not *sous-contrat,* the fees are nevertheless modest at around 520 euros per term for primary school children, and that includes lunches four days a week and *goûter.*

Le Collège et Lycée International Lafayette

23, boulevard Gambetta, Nice. (00 33 4 93 44 75 44, website: www.collegelafayette.com)

This school, also directed by Madame Pascale Rosfelder-Alhadeff, is the secondary school into which École Privée Active Bilingue Le pain de sucre and École Privée Internationale Le pain d'épice feed. The school claims to offer a bilingual education with class sizes from 15 to 20. A third language option (Italian) is offered. The teaching staff includes both French and English mother tongue speakers.

The school accepts children who have not yet learned to speak French on condition that they attend additional classes.

The ABC School

72, boulevard Carnot, 06300 Nice. (00 33 4 92 00 01 23; email abcschool@free.fr; website: www.abcschool.fr)

Despite its name this school caters for children from nursery to age 18. It is a small private non-Catholic school that is *sous-contrat.* Special classes are provided for children who do not speak French very well *(les classes d'adaption).*

Location

The entrance to the school is on a busy main road. There is a school bus that collects from various points in Nice, including the Promenade des Anglais. There is a second bus that starts from Monaco, calling at the Basse Corniche.

School hours

The school is open from 07.45 to 18.00 with the exception of Wednesdays. Classes take place between 09.00 and 16.30.

Fees

School fees are around 500 euros per term, increased to 700 euros per term for children in *les classes d'adaption*. There is a 10% reduction for two children, and a 15% reduction for three.

FRENCH STATE AND PRIVATE SCHOOLS WITH ANGLOPHONE SECTIONS

École Primaire, Sartoux

286, rue de la Vigne Haute, 06560 Valbonne. (00 33 4 93 65 40 66; email primaire.sartoux@wanadoo.fr)

École Primaire, St. Martin

841, chemin de la Plaine, 06250 Mougins. (00 33 4 93 75 51 31; email ecole.0061634U@ac-nice.fr)

The above two primary schools are both French state schools each with an Anglophone section. There is a substantial demand for these places, and early application is advised. For the school in Valbonne, parents must either live in the relevant catchment or work in Valbonne/Sophia Antipolis. For the Mougins school, parents must either live in Mougins or in the neighbouring towns of Cannes, Le Cannet, Mandelieu or Theoule. Application forms can be obtained from the schools (a request by email is sufficient, though you should indicate your child's date of birth). The completed application is sent back to the school along with your child's most recent school reports. There is an entrance test in French and English that takes place in May or June of each year. The headteachers are respectively Madame Rouchette and Monsieur Gyss.

These two schools are associated with the Centre International de Valbonne. However, whilst many children from the two schools go on to the CIV there is no guarantee of a place.

Curriculum

Children at both schools study for about 13 hours per week in each language. Geometry, division and history are studied in French, whereas number skills, geography and science are studied in English.

School hours

The school day starts at 08.30 and finishes at 16.30. After school care is provided until 18.30.

Fees

Parents are required to pay a registration fee of around 250 euros and annual school fees of around 2,400 euros (with reductions for the third and fourth child) to fund the Anglophone teaching.

Centre International de Valbonne (CIV)

190, rue Frederic Mistral. (00 33 4 92 96 52 24; website: www.civfrance.com)

The Centre International de Valbonne is a large French state school under the auspices of the Ministry of Education. It is situated on a huge site in the heart of Sophia Antipolis. It is a secondary school with both a *Collège* and *Lycée* and has five sections: French, Anglo-American, German, Italian and Spanish.

Curriculum

All sections prepare children for the French *brevet* and subsequently the French *Baccalauréat*, with international options. Those in the Anglophone section have the option of taking either the French *Baccalauréat* with an international option or the International Baccalaureate. For children taking the latter option, parents face a huge increase in school fees as this option is entirely private, whereas the former is primarily financed by the French state.

Facilities

The school has a considerable range of facilities including cinema, running track, tennis courts and also for indoor sports.

126

Application process

A considerable number of children from the Anglophone sections of the St. Martin and Mouans Sartoux primary schools go on to continue their education at the CIV, though attendance at these two primary schools is not a guarantee of being accepted to the CIV. Applicants for the CIV, Collège de L'Eganaude and the Collège de Valbonne (see below) are subject to the same entry requirements. They must take written and oral tests in French, maths and the language of the section into which they wish to be admitted. Applications, which can be downloaded from the CIV website, or obtained via the headteacher of your child's primary school, must be submitted between the 1st January and mid-April, and the tests are normally held in the second half of May. The CIV will require your child's school reports for the previous four years. There are no catchment rules as there are with the Anglophone sections in the primary schools, though students are generally allocated to the CIV or one of the colleges according to where they live.

Fees

Attendance at the Italian and Spanish sections is funded by the respective national governments, but parents of children in the Anglophone section must pay to fund the salaries of the English-speaking teaching staff.

Parents pay an annual fee of 1,360 euros for *collège* and 2,020 euros for the *lycée*, with reductions for a third and fourth child.

Boarding accommodation is available in the CIV. This consists of twin and single rooms. Annual boarding fees are in the region of 6,500 euros. A wide range of activities and trips is organised for the

650 boarders. Those interested in boarding should contact Monsieur Audibert or Monsieur Frigo on 00 33 4 92 96 52 04 or 00 33 4 92 96 52 05.

The school's website is well worth visiting, and is packed with information, as is that of ASEICA (see below).

Collège de l'Eganaude

3140, route des Dolines. (00 33 4 97 23 42 20)

An Anglophone section was opened in Eganaude in 2004, and each year a further two classes in a new *sixième* will be added. An Italian section opened in the school at the same time. The school serves primarily the areas of Biot and Sophia Antipolis, but also has students from Cannes, Mougins and Antibes.

Collège de Valbonne
(or College de Niki de St Phalle)

Chemin Darbousson. (00 33 4 92 91 51 30)

This new establishment started admitting students in 2003 and an Anglophone (and also an Italian) section were opened the following year. Most students allocated to this school live in and around Valbonne village.

The Association for the Support of International Education on the Côte d'Azur (ASEICA)

It is this association that employs the English-speaking teachers working in the Anglophone sections of the Centre International de

Valbonne, the College de l'Eganaude, the College de Valbonne and the St. Martin and Haut Sartoux primary schools.

You should consult the association's website www.asseica.org where you will find information on both state primary schools and all three state secondary establishments that have Anglophone sections, much practical information, and details of social and other meetings organised by parents.

Collège Fénélon

122, av. P. Sémard, Grasse. (00 33 4 93 40 60 59; website: www.institut-fenelon.fr)

This is a Catholic French secondary school with a 400-year history. In September 2005 the *collège* opened a *section anglophone.* Accordingly, at the date of writing this section covers the first two years of secondary school each with one class of about 25 pupils. The school is adding a *sixième* class each year. In addition to the *collège*, Fénélon also has a primary school (the headteacher of the primary school is Mr. De Croizals), and a *lycée* though neither has an anglophone section. The *école primaire, collège* and *lycée* are all on different sites in different parts of the town. At present only the *collège* has an international section, though it is anticipated that pupils who complete their education in the *collège* will be catered for in the *lycée.*

Location

The *collège* is at a convenient location, in that if you live south of Grasse, certainly if you are towards Cannes or Mougins, you can reach the school without going through the centre of Grasse. The train station is also only a short walk from the *collège*. There is one rail service only but this is to Cannes and calls at various stations on the way, including Mouans Sartoux.

Children who wish to apply for the Anglophone section must take a short test in English and undergo an interview. The Anglophone section is of course new, and accordingly it is difficult to express any positive views as to the standard of English or of the general education the children will receive. One of the major advantages for parents is that Fénélon provides a more protected and sheltered environment than the Centre International de Valbonne. The school is on a hill and also has a number of steep stairways which could be a problem if your child suffers from a physical disability.

Fees

This is a private school, but as it is *sous-contrat*, fees are in the region of a relatively modest 1,200 euros per year. There is also a small boarding facility at which day pupils are permitted to remain several hours after school.

APPLICATIONS TO FRENCH STATE SCHOOLS

Applications to enter your child into a state nursery school (*maternelle*) or primary school (*école*) should be made directly to the school itself (where there is only one school in the town) or otherwise to your local *mairie*. Applications to *collèges* and *lycées* are handled by the individual schools in conjunction with the Inspection Academique in Nice (04 93 72 63 00).

SCHOOL CHILDREN WITH SPECIAL NEEDS

Details for obtaining financial assistance for children with special needs can be obtained from CDES (Commission Departementale d'Education Speciale) in Nice (04 92 29 43 40).

USEFUL ADDRESSES AND WEBSITES

- www.education.gouv.fr (the French Ministry of Education);

- The English Language Schools Association: 43, rue des Binelles, 92310 Sèvres. (01 45 34 04 11;

- The British Council at www.britishcouncil.fr (see the Education Information Service for details of the main English, American and International schools);

- www.ydelta.free.fr/school.htm;

- www.angloinfo.com.

9
Health Services

British residents on the Côte d'Azur are almost universal in their approval of the standard of health care in France, and are not surprised by the fact that the World Health Organisation placed France at the top of its list for quality of health care. The Alpes-Maritimes has considerably more doctors than the average for the rest of France, with around 3 per 1,000 inhabitants compared to a national average of around 1.9, with the number of dentists and physiotherapists approaching twice the national average.

QUALITY OF CARE

Medical care seems much more accessible on the Côte d'Azur than in the UK. Usually it is possible to arrange to see a consultant within a matter of a few weeks at most, and generally rather sooner. Consultants, and radiographers have premises on the high street. You may have to wait a short time at the surgery before seeing the consultant, or having an x-ray taken, but you do not have to spend hours waiting in a queue, as is often the case in NHS hospitals. Patients have more freedom to change doctors, and perhaps because doctors are conscious of this they tend, in my experience, to be more willing to answer questions, including over the telephone. Other advantages are the number of female consultants, which is higher by far than in the UK. Children tend to receive more specialised care, with most having a paediatrician as the first port of call for medical care, rather than a general practitioner.

PRESSURES ON THE FRENCH HEALTH SYSTEM

Over the past few years, however, the system has shown signs of severe strain. The French use medical services intensively. The level of prescriptions of drugs, including in many cases the unnecessary and even pointless prescription of antibiotics, is extraordinarily high, with the French taking more medication than the residents of any other nation in Europe. The government is taking serious measures. The French have been accused of being preoccupied with their health. The health service is costing the country far too much, and part of this is the astronomic drugs bill and cost of treatment for *le stress*. According to one survey, a third of the French have at some stage taken medication 'for their nerves' with 11% of the participants in the study stating that they had suffered from serious depression in the two weeks prior to the study. The presence of stress is most common amongst the divorced, the unemployed and those on low incomes. Given that the divorce rate is higher on the Côte d'Azur than elsewhere, and the discrepancy between the wealthy and those with modest means is quite striking, it is not surprising that substantial numbers suffer from stress and/or depression.

MÉDECIN TRAITANT

The French health system is beginning to change and in some ways become more like that in the UK. Concerned about the number of unnecessary consultations, the French government has introduced the role of *le médecin traitant.* French residents should register with a particular doctor. To receive the maximum level of reimbursement a patient wishing to see a consultant must now see his *médecin traitant* for a referral. The *médecin traitant* is responsible for co-ordinating the patient's healthcare. A patient can chose to appoint a general practitioner (*médecin généraliste*) as their *médecin traitant,* or any other doctor, such as a consultant from whom they are receiving care for a long-term illness. Parents are not required to appoint a *médecin traitant* for children under 16, but must do so for those aged 16–18. At least one of the child's parents must consent to the choice of *médecin traitant.*

The form for registering with a *médecin traitant* can be downloaded at www.ameli.fr (see *Le formulaire de déclaration du médecin traitant*). There is also a help line open from 08.00 to 20.00 Mon-Fri (0820 77 33 33).

REIMBURSEMENT OF MEDICAL COSTS

Reimbursement is now normally restricted to one consultation with one consultant only. The *médecin traitant* decides which type of specialist for a referral, though the patient may chose which individual specialist to consult.

The obligation to go through your *médecin traitant* to obtain the maximum level of reimbursement does not apply to consultations whilst on holiday, whilst travelling for work purposes, or in a medical emergency. There is no requirement either to obtain a referral in order to consult a dentist, an ophthalmologist or a gynaecologist. If you wish to change *médecin traitant*, you must first obtain the consent of a new doctor, and then inform both the *caisse d'assurance maladie* and your existing doctor. Doctors are not obliged to accept a patient's request to be appointed their *médecin traitant*. They need give no reason for refusal.

CARE FOR THE OLD AND THE INFIRM

One area in which the French system is poor is in relation to nursing care, and help to patients in the community, particularly the aged. There are retirement homes on the Côte d'Azur, but not many. Similarly there are relatively few convalescent homes, or homes for the terminally ill. Often foreign residents in France who are unable to continue to manage alone decide that they have no choice but to return to their native country.

CHILD CARE

Parents receive a *carnet de santé* for each of their children. This is retained by the parent and it should be taken to each medical appointment. Medical staff should record details of treatment, vaccinations, etc. School children are seen by medical professionals whilst at school, including for hearing and sight tests. Parents are given advance notice, and may attend these appointments with their child.

CARE FOR BOTH THE PHYSICALLY AND MENTALLY HANDICAPPED

There is a day centre in Antibes for the mentally handicapped, run by ADAPEI AM, Les Trois Moulins, 656 rue Henri Laugier 06600 Antibes. (04 92 91 40 00) There is also a boarding centre and medical care unit for handicapped children run by the French Red Cross, the Institut Pedagogique les Hirondelles.

MATERNITY SERVICES

Whilst much progress is still needed in the UK in relation to humanising maternity services, the French are generally rather further behind when it comes to allowing women to make their own decisions in relation to care during pregnancy and in deciding their own birth plans. Although most expatriates in France rate the French health system way above that in the UK, maternity care is an exception. Maternity care in France remains very 'medicalised', rather like the UK of the 1970s. Expectant mothers are followed by an obstetrician from the outset, and have numerous scans throughout the pregnancy. Midwives play much less of a role in prenatal care. This is even more marked following the birth – there is no system of community midwives as in the UK.

There is now at least one British midwife practising in the region, Vivienne Rion who is based in the Var (04 94 67 41 25). Once a pregnancy is confirmed a woman should receive a *carnet de maternité* in which medical staff will record the progress of the pregnancy. The booklet also contains practical information.

HOSPITAL CARE

The main hospitals on the Côte d'Azur are unsurprisingly in Nice. The largest hospital is L'Archet. Lenvale, on the Promenade des Anglais is the city's children's hospital. A parent wishing to stay overnight with a child can ask for a *chambre mère-enfant*. This costs around €45, including meals. Sadly patients the world over, especially children, are always at risk from intruders breaching often inadequate security, from other child and adult patients, and even those responsible for their medical and nursing care.

One matter that you should be aware of is that private hospitals, even highly reputable ones, have been suspected of 'bending the rules' to inflate their claims for reimbursement by the state, sometimes by prolonging a patient's stay in hospital, or allocating an outpatient a room for the day when this is really not necessary.

Each year the magazine *Le Point* publishes a list of France's best hospitals. In last year's survey only the Centre Hospitalier Universitaire de Nice made the top 20, coming in at 13th.

PREVENTATIVE HEALTH CARE

The 'flu vaccine is widely available and free to those over 65, and those suffering from respiratory problems and diabetes.

The authorities have an established programme for breast screening (see www.rendezvoussanteplus.net).

CHEMISTS (*PHARMACIES*)

Pharmacists operate a duty rota 24 hours a day, seven days a week. You should find details of the out-of-hours pharmacist in the windows of pharmacies, and in the local newspaper. You will generally have to attend a manned police station before attending a pharmacy out of hours. The police will telephone the pharmacists to inform them you will be calling.

ENGLISH-SPEAKING DOCTORS

As medical appointments are very important, make sure that your French doctor really does understand exactly what you mean. You can obtain assistance by:

- consulting the British consulate in Marseille which keeps a list of the doctors known to speak English;

- contacting your private health insurer which may also have a similar list;

- consulting the websites of the local English-speaking press.

A relatively recent innovation is Riviera Medical Services, an emergency medical service (04 93 26 12 70). Another service is Doctors on Call (Nice) 04 93 52 42 42.

YOUR RIGHTS TO MEDICAL COVER AND TREATMENT

Visitors

The European Health Insurance Card (EHIC) (*Carte européene d'assurance maladie* [*CEAM*]), available from your local *Caisse d'assurance* in France, or in the UK from your local post office or at www.ehic.org.uk, entitles you not only to emergency treatment, but also necessary routine medical treatment for a temporary period of up to 12 months spent in France or any other EU country. You will have to pay for your medical treatment and apply for reimbursement of the major part of the costs incurred, when you return to the UK.

Working in France

Those working in France must normally participate in the French social security system. Employers are required to register new employees with the social security authorities. They must also deduct social security contributions from your salary. If your household income is less than 6,965 euros p.a. you are entitled to health cover (*Couverture Maladie Universelle*, or *CMU*) without charge. Otherwise you are required to contribute 8% of your declared income. See the website www.ameli.fr for further details.

UK nationals sent to work in France by their employer temporarily, are covered under the French health system provided their UK National Insurance contributions continue to be paid. The relevant E-form is the E106. This should be completed and sent to you by the UK authorities and you should then take it to your local *caisse primaire d'assurance maladie*. You should request that they record details of your dependants on the form. People who live and work in the UK, but whose families are resident in France, will need to obtain Form E109. The position for the retired is set out in Chapter 6.

LA CARTE VITALE

This electronic card is issued to residents over 16 and should be produced whenever you use medical services. Using the card means that you should receive your entitlement to reimbursement direct into your bank account within five days without completing any forms. The card contains details of your health rights, your name and address and it is anticipated that patients' medical history will be added in the near future. Patients will control who can have access to that information, but will be penalised in the extent to which their expenses are reimbursed if they restrict their medical advisers' access to this information. You should contact Le Service Relations Internationales in Nice to obtain your *Carte Vitale* (06180 Nice Cedex 2. (04 92 09 42 64)

RATES OF REIMBURSEMENT

The standard fee for consultations with a general practitioner *médecin traitant* is €20, 70% of which is reimbursed less the €1 *de participation forfaitaire*, i.e. €13, by the *sécurité sociale*. An appointment with a consultant involves a standard fee of €25, of which €16.50 is reimbursed. You may prefer to have a private consultation to obtain an earlier consultation or a consultation with a particular doctor. This will typically cost you more than twice the standard fee. You will only be able to recover reimbursement equivalent to that appropriate to the standard fee i.e. €16.50. Those with the benefit of a *mutuelle* will obviously receive a greater amount of total reimbursement. Reimbursement of dental and orthodontic care is very limited.

Reimbursement of hospital bills is 100% and handled by the

hospitals. You will not be required to pay. This complete reimbursement embraces antenatal care and childbirth, surgery, and treatment for long-term illness. In-patients pay a *forfait journalier*, currently €14, for meals. Post-operative outpatient care, however, is only reimbursed at the rate of 65%.

LA MUTUELLE AND PRIVATE INSURANCE

Residents in France entitled to cover under the French social security system should consider taking out a *mutuelle* to cover those costs not met by the French social security system. Several companies provide health insurance cover (e.g. Exclusive Health Care, website: www.exclusivehealthcare.com). Care is needed in choosing the level of cover provided. Policies vary in the extent to which patients can choose doctors and hospitals, and on matters that are excluded from cover.

EMERGENCY TELEPHONE NUMBERS:
- SAMU (Service d'Aide Médicale Urgence): 15
- Police : 17
- Fire: 18

Emergency numbers using your mobile phone:
- SOS Medecins d'Antibes: 0825 06 70 00
- SOS Medecins Cannes: 0825 00 50 04
- SOS Medecins Nice: 0810 85 01 01
- SOS Medecins Fréjus: 04 94 95 15 25

141

Emergency numbers for children:

- L'Archet Nice: 04 92 03 60 89
- Lenval Nice: 04 92 03 03 03
- Hôpital d'Antibes: 04 92 91 77 98
- Hôpital de Cannes: 04 93 69 71 50
- Hôpital de Clavary in Grasse: 04 93 09 55 04
- Hôpital Fréjus: 04 94 40 20 83

10

Shops, services, social groups and activities for English speakers

Apart from perhaps the French capital, the Alpes-Maritimes has a higher concentration of English speakers than any other area in France. There are accordingly more facilities for the Anglophone communities than elsewhere, with many British people being employed in the businesses that provide them.

SHOPS

There are a number of outlets selling British food and other products.

- Geoffrey's of London at La Galerie du Port, rue Lacan 06600 Antibes. (04 93 34 55 70; www.geoffreysoflondon.com). Geoffrey's also sells some Irish and American products.

- Brittain's Home Stores, at the Forum Roudabout, 1913 Route de Cannes, Valbonne (04 93 42 01 70; www.brittains-stores.com). This store has the advantage of being at a convenient driving distance from the British and International Schools in the

Sophia Antipolis area and having good parking facilities.

Some of the French supermarkets have a small selection of British items, including:

- Champion in Mougins and Antibes;
- Carrefour in Antibes (04 92 91 25 25);
- Marché-U in Beaulieu-sur-Mer (04 93 01 04 61);
- Galeries Lafayette in Cap 3000 at St. Laurent-du-Var.

Indeed Geoffrey Garnet of Geoffrey's of London announced last year that he had reached agreements with 70 supermarkets that they would allocate space to stock British-type goods, to be supplied by him from his base in Antibes.

As to the large British chains, Virgin Megastore has a branch in Nice, and the Bodyshop has branches in Nice Etoile and Cap 3000.

ENGLISH LANGUAGE BOOKSHOPS

There is a good selection of English language bookshops on the Côte d'Azur, all of them well-established.

The oldest, having opened its doors in 1980, is Scruples on rue Princesse Caroline in Monaco (00 377 93 50 43 52).

The largest is Antibes Books, 24 rue Aubernon in Antibes 04 93 34 74 11), which in addition to stocking a wide range of new books also has a selection of second hand books.

The Cat's Whiskers at 30 rue Lamartine in Nice (04 93 80 02 66) has a range of English teaching materials.

Other bookshops in the region include:

- The Cannes English Bookshop, rue Bivouac-Napoleon (04 93 34 45 66) only a short walk from the Palais des Festivals;

- The English Book Centre, 12 rue Alexis Julien in Valbonne (04 93 12 21 42);

- The Castle Bookshop at 1 rue Saint Pierre in Fayence (04 94 84 72 00);

- Heidi's Bookshop in Villecroze, Draguignan.

If you are new to the area, the English bookshops are well worth a visit. Apart from being able to pick up copies of *The Riviera Times* and *The Anglophone Book* it is well worth chatting to the proprietors and their staff. They often have noticeboards with useful information and the faciltiies for you to put up your own advertisement.

It is also possible, of course, to order books to be delivered to your address in France from www.amazon.co.uk, or from www.amazon.fr. Indeed, if you already have an account at Amazon.co.uk, this will also work with Amazon.fr.

BANKING

British banks represented in the area include Barclays, with currently a large billboard to welcome you to Nice airport and branches in Nice (04 93 82 68 00), Antibes, Cannes, Cagnes-sur-Mer and Menton.

Banque Populaire Côte d'Azur has 85 branches in the Alpes-Maritimes, Var and Monaco and offers banking services in English, centralised from their Nice branch. Contact Marion Courtonne, Simon Moore and Graeme Mackay on 04 93 82 81 80 or see the website www.cotedazur.banquepopulaire.fr.

BNP Paribas, which took over Abbey National France in 2005 also has a team specifically catering for English speakers, as does Credit Immobilier that took over the Woolwich some years previously.

Crédit Agricole has recently started an international section based at its regional headquarters at St. Laurent-du-Var.

TAKEAWAY INDIAN FOOD

Takeaway food options include Curry and Spice – an Indian meal brought to your doorstep usually within an hour of you placing your order (www.curryandspice.com; 06 14 66 12 24). The service extends to St. Raphael in the west and to Menton in the east.

DOCTORS AND DENTISTS

As to doctors and dentists, many of those practising in the Alpes-Maritimes speak some English.

There is a British General Practitioner not far from Mougins: Dr. Ireland (04 93 12 95 66).

British dentists include Helen Giacommi in Cagnes-sur-Mer (04 93 22 92 77) and Robert Hempleman in Cannes (04 93 38 10 83).

The French orthodontist Dr. Dossou in rue d'Antibes in Cannes underwent orthodontic training in both France and the United

States and has a number of English-speaking clients.

Optician Albert Seroussi, 40 Bd Marechal Juin, Cagnes-sur-Mer (04 93 20 75 12) and osteopath, Nik 251 chemin des Gourettes, Mouans Sartoux (04 92 28 51 75) also welcome English speakers.

THE SUNNYBANK RETIREMENT HOME

For over a century the Sunnybank Hospital in Cannes served as a kind of 'cottage hospital' for residents and visitors to the French Riviera. The hospital closed in 1997, and the land was sold off. The proceeds of sale are under the control of a committee headed by retired banker Peter Durlacher, and including two local general practitioners Patrick Ireland and Mark Brunelli. A decision was made to establish an English-speaking retirement home with medical facilities. A new site was purchased in Mouans-Sartoux and it is anticipated that the home will have around 80 beds in well-equipped rooms as well as restaurants and guest rooms.

This is scheduled to open in 2007. In an early survey carried out in 2004 as many as three hundred people expressed a serious interest.

For further information telephone Peter Durlacher (04 93 90 02 16; peter.durance@wanadoo.fr).

CHURCHES

Anglican

There are a considerable number of Anglican churches along the Riviera, providing not only a community in which to worship, but also a focal point for social, cultural and other activities amongst English-speakers and, indeed, other nationalities. Currently there are the following Anglican churches:

- Holy Trinity, Cannes, behind the Carlton Hotel (04 93 94 54 61);

- Holy Trinity, Nice rue de la Buffa (04 93 87 19 83);

- St Michael's Church, Beaulieu-sur-Mer (04 93 01 46 51);

- St. John's Church, Menton (04 93 57 20 25);

- St. John's Church, St. Raphael (04 94 95 45 78);

- Grimaud Village Church (04 94 95 45 78);

- St. Hugh's Church, Vence (04 93 87 19 83);

- St. Paul's Anglican Church in Monaco (00 377 93 30 71 06);

- Seillans Parish Church (04 94 51 16 98) in the Var.

Non-Anglican

There is a non-Anglican Christian Fellowship group that meets in Sophia Antipolis – the Cornerstone Christian Fellowship. It is a lively bilingual protestant church with a children's Sunday school and nursery. For further information see www.c-stone.org or telephone 04 92 38 98 91.

There are also non-conformist international churches in Cannes and Nice.The International Baptist Church in Nice meets at 13 rue Vernier (04 93 24 92 61), and that in St. Paul can be contacted on 04 93 77 31 45.

For further details in relation to places of worship see www.angloinfo.com or www.rivierareporter.com or telephone the

British Consulate in Marseille (see Appendices for contact details).

SOURCES OF INFORMATION IN ENGLISH

A very useful source of information and advice is the association Adapt in France, Tel: 04 93 65 33 79 (see Chapter 1 for more information on this association) based in Sophia Antipolis. There are different rates of membership fees payable, depending on your requirements. It is well used by English speakers, has a library of resources, and runs over a dozen different workshops on topics such as working in France, setting up a business, schooling, etc. Information can be obtained by consulting www.adaptinfrance.org.

Another particularly helpful website, packed with information in English, is www.amb-cotedazur.com.

ASSOCIATIONS

The British Association

There are numerous clubs and associations in the Alpes-Maritimes run for and by English-speaking expatriates, ranging from amateur dramatics, to rugby and cricket, to party political groups. Perhaps the longest established is the British Association with branches in Cannes (04 93 97 33 02), Menton (04 92 10 28 11), Monaco (00 377 93 50 19 52), Nice (04 93 24 84 90) and the Var (04 94 72 79 34). The Association organises a calendar of social, cultural and fund-raising events, produces regular newsletters packed with practical information and will provide advice and assistance (in appropriate cases even financial assistance) to British people living in the area. The British Association in the Var offers French conversation classes. It has provided a substantial role in helping those who have suffered from the summer forest fires in the department.

Singing, theatre, dance, etc.

These include:

• The Purcell Chamber Choir (04 93 75 57 47);

• The Red Pear Theatre Antibes (04 93 74 72 17);

• The Riviera Amateur Dramatic Association (04 93 77 99 59);

• The Monaco Drama Group (06 16 36 59 05);

• The Ensemble Vocal Syrinx (04 93 20 68 94);

• The Riviera Dance Club based in Mouans Sartoux (06 26 01 50 70);

• The Scottish Dance Group of Monaco (00 377 93 25 18 49);

• Scottish Dancing Côte d'Azur (04 93 42 72 95).

Social

These include:

• The Auld Alliance (04 93 08 32 78);

• The International Women's Club of the Var (04 94 76 33 76);

• The Women's Club of the Riviera (04 93 01 24 48);

• Women's Friendship Club, Monaco (00 377 93 30 71 06) and Riviera Singles (04 93 32 89 78).

The Anglo-American Group of Provence (AAGP) also has an extremely wide range of activities (01 42 53 04 07).

Sport

There are now at least five cricket clubs spread across the south of France:

- Monte Carlo (06 63 47 11 86);

- Cabris (04 93 70 27 23);

- Entrecasteaux (04 94 04 42 13);

- Provence/Aix (04 42 21 99 02);

- Montpellier (04 67 58 83 63, or contact Nigel Wynn on 04 67 86 69 19).

Other sports associations include The Menton Tennis Club, and the Riviera Expat Golf Society.

Commonwealth

- The Commonwealth Club (06 14 66 12 24);

- The Australian Club (06 84 24 07 65);

- The Canadian Club (04 93 77 53 12);

- Canadians Together (06 64 61 37 35; www.canadiens-sur-la-cote.org);

- The South African Club (06 61 85 15 27).

Speak French and/or meet the French

The most well-established association providing a common meeting point for French and English is the Association France–Grande-Bretagne. Both the Nice and Cannes branches hold French conversation classes and arrange regular social and cultural events. Other groups include the Riviera Franglais Club (06 62 25 19 67) aimed at encouraging expatriates to meet French people and speak the language. It arranges a wide selection of events from barbecues to hiking, sailing and eating out.

In addition there is The Forum (06 16 81 90 90; 04 93 74 76 54) and the Amities franco-Anglophones, now in its tenth year, which meets twice a week in Menton at the Terminus café-restaurant opposite the train station.

Café International meets in Espace Magnan in Nice on Monday evenings from 18.00 to 20.00 and insists on participants using two languages (www.espacemagnan.com; 04 93 97 04 30).

Other European

- The Dutch Club (04 93 09 86 97; 04 93 66 24 93), now in its 45th year with 2,000 members;
- The Finnish Association (06 03 84 62 05) with over 300 members;
- Danish Club (04 93 58 32 77);
- Swedish Club (04 92 13 15 35; 04 93 20 40 64);
- The Cercle Nordique (04 93 34 55 59);
- Danish Lutheran Church in Beaulieu-sur-Mer (04 93 21 07 02);
- Swedish Church in Cagnes-sur-Mer (04 93 20 40 64).

University and professional

These include the Oxbridge Set (Oxford, Cambridge and Trinity College, Dublin – 00 377 93 50 74 18) and The Franklin Club, 16 rue Henri Germain, 06210 Le Cannet (06 93 43 56 27). The latter is an association of retired executives that organises social and cultural events. Anyone who has held a position with some responsibility can join. Another professional social group is Sophia Professional Women's Network (www.spwn.net).

Armed forces

There are branches of the Royal British Legion in Nice (04 93 01 30 00) and Cannes (04 93 64 29 79) and a branch of the Royal Air Force Association in the Alpes-Maritimes (04 94 79 76 39).

FILMS IN ENGLISH

English films can be seen at most major cinemas with French subtitles (described as *version originale* or *V.O.*). In addition a regular programme of films in English can be seen at the Sporting Hiver, Place du Casino, Monte Carlo. You can find out details of their programme at www.cinemasporting.com or telephone 08 92 68 00 72.

PRIVATE LESSONS

Music

Piano, violin and viola: Erin Skehan (04 93 12 26 73).

Driving

Fehrenbach International Driving School (including 'defensive' driving): (04 93 07 58 90; www.frenchlicense.com).

Computing

- Anna Carlier, Computer Training and Development (annacarlier@yahoo.co.uk);

- Absolute Beginners Computer Courses based in Sophia Antipolis (04 93 40 82 33).

ENGLISH-SPEAKING ELECTRICIAN

English-speaking electricians working on the coast include Jean-Francois Fontaine (www.elecgen.com).

ENGLISH LIBRARIES

The most substantial is probably the English-American library. Located in the basement of the church hall of the Holy Trinity Anglican Church in Nice off rue de la Biffa, the library dates from 1862. It has a stock of around 24,000 books and offers a number of membership schemes suitable for holiday makers and residents.

Most residents using the library opt for the 28 euros annual subscription that enables them to take out up to four books (or eight paperbacks) at any one time. There is a wide range of books, including fiction and travel books, both old and contemporary. The library also stocks videos and English newspapers and is run by a team of volunteers. It is open on Tuesday, Wednesday, Thursday and Saturday from 10.00–11.00 and 15.00–17.00, and on Friday from 15.00–17.00. Contact Judit on 06 16 56 50 35 or 04 93 16 96 49.

The main other English language libraries in the region are in Vence (04 93 58 97 71) and in Monaco (The Princess Grace Irish Library, 9 rue Princesse Marie-de-Lorraine 00 377 93 50 12 25). The Holy Trinity Church in Cannes also has a library.

Further afield there is a library in Malaucène, in Vaucluse (the Beaumont Library 04 90 65 25 60).

ENGLISH LANGUAGE MAGAZINES, NEWSPAPERS AND RADIO STATIONS

There are several English language magazines and newspapers. New publications appear from time to time, though in many cases go out of business after only a few months or years. The longest established is the *Riviera Reporter* that also has an extremely useful website www.rivierareporter.com. Other established publications include the *Riviera Times*. The most popular English language radio station is *Riviera Radio* whose website is also well worth a visit, www.rivieraradio.mc. Other stations broadcasting to the area include *The Breeze*, and *Radio International*.

In the Var a useful source of information is the website of *Var Village Voice*, the local English language newspaper (www.varvillagevoice.com; 04 94 04 49 60).

MARSEILLE BRITISH CONSULATE'S EMAILING LIST

It is worthwhile asking to go onto the Marseille British consulate's emailing list (contact Pascale.Gauthier-Keogh@fco.gov.uk). You will receive details of a host of social and other events throughout Provence.

11
Leisure time on the Côte d'Azur

Nice is an excellent base not only for coastal resorts and beaches, water sports and opportunities to see marine life such as dolphins swimming parallel to the coast roads, but also for hiking in the nearby mountains, and skiing in the winter season. The region boasts several river valleys (L'Esterel, La Siagne, Le Loup, Le Var, La Vesubie, Le Paillon, La Bevera) providing ample choice for kayak, rafting and canyoning. There are nearly 30 golf courses in the Alpes-Maritimes and the Var.

BEACHES

Pollution

Swimmers should ensure that after a dip in the sea they take a thorough wash under one of the numerous showers dotted along the coast. The waters suffer from varying degrees of pollution and chemical and bacterial pollutants can cause skin rashes, stomach upsets or ear infections. Never swim in the sea after it has been raining, as the polluted rainfall significantly increases the chances of developing health problems from swimming in the sea. As always when swimming, never do so after a heavy meal.

Blue flag

Some of the Riviera's beaches have been award a blue flag. Do not assume that this means that you can bathe in safety – it is simply a recognition given to those resorts that are making an effort to keep their coastlines clean. Blue flag beaches can be found in the Varat:

- Hyeres-les-Palmiers;
- La Croix Valmar;
- Saint-Mandrier;
- Sainte-Maxime;
- Le Lavandou;
- Le Pradet.

And in the Alpes-Maritimes at:

- Antibes;
- Cap d'Ail.

Tents and caravans are forbidden on beaches, as are barbecues. French law provides that the public have right to unrestricted and free access to all beaches, permitting members of the public to walk through private beaches, or swim in the water. Some of those 'policing' the private beaches often use threatening tactics to discourage people from exercising this right.

Notable resorts include Théoule-sur-Mer, the French winner of a European award for tourism. It is worth advancing a little further towards the Var to the fairly peaceful beaches at Miramar. Other beaches well worth visiting are those at Juan les Pins, St. Jean Cap Ferrat, Menton and Port Grimaud.

Sports on the beach and in the sea

A number of beaches have facilities for volleyball, such as those along the Promenade des Anglais in Nice, namely on the Plage Publique des Ponchettes and the Plage Publique de Carras. Antibes has one beach on which you can play volleyball, as does Cannes (on the Mandelieu La Napoule side). At Saint-Tropez volleyball is played on the Plage des Salins. Most of the resorts along the coast have facilities for windsurfing, sailing, and water-skiing. Parasailing is available in Cannes and Nice, and jet skiing in Nice and Antibes.

Naturist beaches

Les Alpes-Maritimes boasts only one beach on which you can tan where the sun does not usually shine: at La Batterie between Cannes and Golf-Juan.

If you do not like La Batterie, put your clothes back on and head west into the Var where you will find a much greater selection, including beaches at:

- Le Lavender (Ile du Levant and Le Layet-Cavaliere);
- Cavaliere (Cap Negre, Nasque);
- St. Rapael (Cap Dramont, Petite Vaquette);
- Ramatuelle (Plage de Pampelonne, Cap Taillat).

If you are really enthusiastic you could even join the Federation Française de Naturisme (www.ffn-naturisme.com).

THE REGION'S LAKES

There are many lakes away from the coast where you can savour the region's beauty in a quieter and cooler setting than along the coast. The nearest are some of the 160 lakes in the Mercantour Park that extends over both the department of les Alpes-Maritimes and that of les Alpes-de-Haute Provence. The lakes are not accessible by car, and are particularly favoured by hikers. Of particular note are Lac d'Allos, which is about half an hour's walk from the parking area near the village of Allos, and Lac de Vens. To the east is the very popular and easily accessible Lac St-Cassien only a short drive from the A8 exit at Les Adrets in the Var. If you want to travel a little further into the Var you could visit the four lakes of the Gorges de Verdun. These lakes offer a variety of water sports, as does Lac St. Cassien, including windsurfing and pedal boats.

Mercantour National Park

In 2005 a new multi-million euro project opened on the edge of the Mercantour National Park. The wolf-park at Le Boreon is expected to attract 60,000 visitors in 2006. When it opened in July 2005 there was only a handful of wolves, but it is hoped that the sanctuary and tourist attraction will eventually be home to up to 60 wolves. There are believed to be 30–40 wild wolves living in the French Alps, many having crossed over the border from Italy. The centre is about an hour and a half from Nice in the depths of the region's forests. It would be possible to combine a visit to the centre with a hike in the surrounding countryside, for example in the Salese Valley. This area is very sparsely populated, save by wild life such as marmots, ibex and birds of prey.

Prices for the centre are 9 euros for adults, 7 euros for children.

HORSE RACING

The Hippodrome de la Côte d'Azur in Cagnes-sur-Mer (www.hippodrome-cotedazur.com) is one of the busiest race courses in France in terms of the number of race meetings each year.

SKIING

The two nearest resorts are those of Isola and Auron, though if you are prepared to travel further those at Courchevel are particularly suitable for beginners or those less accomplished, with superb hotels and chalets, and plenty of English-speaking ski-instructors. You can find further information at www.courchevel.com. Another favourite is Val d'Isere which has slopes to suit a range of abilities (see www.valdisere.com for more details).

An alarming number of skiers suffer injuries each year. You can obviously reduce the risk by getting into shape before hitting the ski slopes, only using good and well-maintained equipment, and respecting hazard signs.

Insurance is a must. Standard health insurance policies often do not cover skiing accidents. Even if you have health cover under the French health system, this will not pay for the cost of evacuating you from the slopes, which could easily cost 2,000 to 3,000 euros or more. You can purchase insurance on the slopes in the form of a *carte neige,* or take out a policy in advance (such as that offered by AXA), or join a ski club and insure through their group policy. Take care to ascertain the precise level of cover offered, and the exclusions.

For information on the risk of avalanches see www.meteo.fr/meteonet_en/services/prc.htm.

DAY TRIPS

Aix-en-Provence, only two and a quarter hours from Nice, is a particularly attractive university city, that has been likened to Oxford. The city has a significant and quite close-knit though welcoming Anglophone community, many of whom are members of the Anglo-American Group of Provence. There is a direct coach link from Nice to Aix that stops at Le Cannet and Mandelieu.

The Italian Riviera is also within easy distance for a day trip, as are the Îles de Lérins, with crossings from Cannes and Mandelieu.

CULTURE IN NICE

The city itself is generously stocked with cultural sites including 19 museums and galleries, two large theatres and several smaller ones, an opera, a symphony orchestra as well as four chamber orchestras, and no fewer than 27 libraries.

RESTAURANTS

Those not far from the A8 motorway in the Var or Alpes-Maritimes who enjoy a traditional fish and chip supper should pay a visit to Jim Cookson at Les Arbousiers restaurant (04 93 60 67 89), situated on the shores of Lac St. Cassien, a short drive from exit 39. You can swim in this large lake or hire a pedal boat.

Another English run establishment, worth a visit for a traditional Sunday lunch, is Le Relais des Coches in Tourrettes-sur-Loup (04 93 24 30 24). It offers stunning views of the village and the Mediterranean coast, excellent traditional English roasts, and a crackling log fire in the winter.

Further restaurants worth visiting include:

- The Grimaldi Hotel in the Place du Chateau, Cagnes-sur-Mer (04 93 20 60 24). Menus at 32 euros and 52 euros. The Risotto de la Riviera is said to be delicious.

- Le Valbonnais Route de Biot, Valbonne (04 93 12 03 84). A good value restaurant serving pizzas and pasta, salads and grills. A hearty meal will cost you less than 20 euros a head. Booking advisable.

- Le Safari in Cours Saleya, Nice (04 93 80 18 44). Situated at the east end of the market area this lively, friendly restaurant has quite a large terrace. The menu includes pizzas and pasta as well as a selection of local dishes including fresh fish.

- Café des Arcades, Valbonne (04 93 12 00 06). Located in the central square it also serves a selection of local dishes, pizzas, pasta and grills.

For commentaries on a selection of 800 restaurants in the Alpes-Maritimes, Var, Bouches-du-Rhone, the Vaucluse and Monaco see the *Guide Gantie* (available from good bookshops and on line at www.guidegantie.com).

EVENING ENTERTAINMENT

Live music venues include Morrison's and Quays in Cannes, O'Sullivan's in Mandelieu, and Check Point, Distilleries Ideales, King's Pub, Ma Nolan's, McMahon's, Paddy's Pub, Thor, Wayne's and 3 Diables all in Nice. For those intent on pub crawls, theme parties and regular gigs, see the *Complete Guide to Funky Riviera* at www.funkymaps.com (06 98 15 44 55).

HOLIDAYS FROM NICE

A good starting point for your holidays departing from Nice airport is the airport's associated website www.plaisirdepartir.com in partnership with around 40 tour operators and over 100 travel agents. The brochure is available at various locations in both airport terminals. Information is also available on 08 20 42 33 33 (0.12 euros per minute). Bookings made via the website carry an entitlement to special parking rates at the airport's car parks.

12
Activities for children

Children arc particularly well catered for in the region and some of the many attractions are listed below.

THEME PARKS

- Koaland, parc d'attractions. 5 avenue de la Madone, Menton. Specially suited for children aged 2–7. Jungle, go-karting, minigolf. (04 92 10 00 40)

- San Estello, Domaine de Barbossi, 3300 route de Fréjus Mandelieu, RN7. Merry-go-rounds, pony rides, small farm, trampolines, mini-golf. Particularly suitable for younger children. Tennis lessons. (04 93 49 64 74)

- Antibes Land (opposite Marineland in Antibes). Over 20 different attractions. (04 93 33 68 03)

- Aqua-Splash Marineland in Antibes. 12 giant slides, wave pool, giant pool, pool for younger children. Open summer only. (04 93 33 49 49)

- Aquatica, Fréjus. Water leisure park open every day from June to September. (04 94 51 82 51)

- Marineland, Antibes. Sharks, dolphins, whales, otters. Evening shows during the summer. Free for children under 3. Situated on the RN 7 in Antibes (www.marineland.fr; 04 93 33 49 49).

- Laser Quest 81, rue Albert Einstein, Zone Industrielle La Palud, Fréjus. A labyrinth of action where children can shoot each other over and over again. (04 94 17 08 28). Also in Cannes, La Bocca (04 93 47 50 90).

- Ferme de St. Pierre, Bargème in the Haut Var. A fun learning experience for younger children who can see a wide range of farm animals at close quarters. It is also possible to stay overnight (04 94 84 21 55).

BEACH CLUBS (*CLUBS DE PLAGE*)

- Le Club Mickay, Cagnes-sur-Mer (04 93 22 83 20)

- La plage privée du Majestic, Cannes (04 92 98 77 00)

- A new park opened not long ago in Villeneuve-Loubet, le Granouillou Park with a wide variety of inflatable structures (06 09 53 35 98)

MUSEUMS MORE SUITED TO CHILDREN

- The Oceanographic Museum in Monaco has over 6,000 fish and invertebrates, and a huge skeleton of a whale. (00 377 93 15 36 00)

- Musée de Paléontologie Humaine de Terra Amata, 25 Boulevard Carnot in Nice is well worth a visit, especially during the school holidays when there are free workshops. (04 93 55 59 93)

- L'Observatoire de Nice, Boulevard de l'Observatoire, Nice (04 92 00 30 11)

TRIPS AT SEA

- Les Îles de Lérins (Ile Sainte Marguerite and Ile Saint Honorat) are well worth a visit. Boats leave from Cannes, Golfe-Juan and also Mandelieu la Napoule (30 minutes). The Musée de la Mer on Ile Sainte-Marguerite houses the cell where the Man in the Iron Mask was imprisoned.

- Underwater submarine trips around Cap d'Antibes lasting about one hour on the Visiobulle from April to the end of September. Departs from Juan-les-Pins. Reservation recommended. (04 93 67 02 11)

ICE SKATING

The ice rinks on the Côte d'Azur are:

- Patinoire du Palais des Sports in Nice, open all year round. (04 93 80 80 80);

- Club de Monaco, open from December to March. (00 377 93 30 64 83);

- Patinoire Naturelle d'Isola 2000 (04 93 23 15 15).

TENNIS

- Lessons at Tennis Club de l'Argentière, bd de la Tavernière, behind the Géant in Mandelieu, five minutes from the A8 motorway junction with parking, two minutes from the resort of Mandelieu-La Napoule and ten minutes from Théoule-sur-Mer. (04 93 93 03 03)

- Tennis Club Les Oiseaux, avenue Notre dame de Viel (not far from Mougins junction of A8). This municipal sports centre is well maintained, and attractive. Open to those not resident in Mougins. (04 92 92 59 94)

- Tennis Club, 14 rue Albert 1er Menton. (04 93 57 85 85)

- Sophia Country Club, 3550 route des Dollines. Annual membership 160 euros. (04 92 96 68 86)

GO-KARTING

- Cannes Formule Karting on the RN7 215 avenue Francis Tonner Cannes-La-Bocca. Children from seven years old. (04 93 47 88 88)

- Fun Kart, Plateau de la Sarrée, route de Gourdon (the D3), Bar-sur-Loup. Also has mini-golf, archery, table tennis and boules. Open every day of the year, for adults and children from five years old. (04 93 42 48 08)

- Buggy Cross. Quads and bikes. Open air. Near the Car Museum towards Mougins. The Car museum is easily accessible from the A8 (going towards Nice) and you can park in the museum car park and walk to Buggy Cross. Otherwise this attraction can be a little difficult to find if you are not familiar with the area. (04 93 69 02 74)

FIRST FLYING LESSONS

Adolescents from age 12 can take a first flight accompanied by a professional pilot at Cannes-Mandelieu airport. Twenty minutes costs around 60 euros. (04 93 47 64 43)

ZOOS

- Parc Zoologique de Fréjus. www.zoo-frejus.com. Visit is partly on foot, partly in your car. Open all year round from 10.30–16.30. Take exit 38 of the A8. (04 98 11 37 37)

- Le Village des Tortues at Gonfaron in the Var. Animal park with giant tortoises. Open from 1st March to the end of November. (04 94 78 26 41)

- Zoo du Cap Ferrat (tigers, monkeys, bears, zebras, crocodiles). (04 93 76 07 60)

CAVES

At Saint Vallier de Thiey, 20 minutes from Grasse you can visit stunning caves some 70 metres underground with stalactites and stalagmites. (04 93 42 61 63)

PARKS AND OPEN PLACES

- Parc Floral Phoenix, promcnade des Anglais, Nice. Exhibitions and activities, aquarium, exotic butterflies. (04 92 29 77 00)

- La Valmasque. This wooded area around Cannes, Mougins, Valbonne and Antibes is ideal for walks.

TOY SHOPS

- Pierrot la Lune (for very young children) 8, rue James Close, Vieil Antibes. (04 93 34 16 00)

- One of the largest and best toy shops on the coast is Contesso at 16 avenue Notre Dame in the centre of Nice. (04 93 85 43 10)

Other toyshops include La Grande Recree in the Tourrades in Mandelieu and Nice Etoile and Le Joué Club that has shops in Cannes, Antibes, Grasse, Nice and Vence. There is a Toys R Us at the Lingoustière centre, Route de Grenoble outside Nice. (04 93 18 11 18)

CHILDREN'S CLOTHES SHOPS

There are a considerable number of boutiques, such as Petit Bâteau in Nice, and Cap 3000 in Saint Laurent-du-Var, and Le Shop at 37 rue Droite 06300 in Vieux Nice, where you can buy clothes for young children. They tend to be quite expensive. It is worthwhile visiting one of the three branches of Du Pareil au Même on the coast at Cannes (2 rue Maréchal Foch), Antibes (12 bis rue Championnet) and Nice (44 rue Pastorelli) where there is a good selection of quite fashionable clothes at modest prices for the under 12s.

SICK AND HANDICAPPED CHILDREN

La Maison de Bonheur helps children with terminal illnesses and their families. 17, rue de l'hôtel des Postes. (04 93 80 89 42)

Organisations providing sporting events or courses for handicapped children include:

- L'Association Culture Sport Adapté in Antibes (04 92 91 19 01);

- Club des handicapés sportif Azureens, Les Collines du Capitou Mandelieu. (04 93 45 43 89)

LES CENTRES DE LOISIRS

- **Cagnes-sur-Mer**: Boulevard de la Plage (04 93 07 33 04). Welcomes teenagers from age 13 upwards. École Pain du Sucre (04 93 73 70 41) for children from age 2.

- **Cannes**: Ferme Giaume, 7 avenue Coubertin, for 11–16-year-olds. (04 93 47 06 33)

- **Menton**: Base Nautique, promenade de mer for 4–11-year-olds. (04 93 35 49 70)

- **Mougins**: Complex Sportif des Oiseaux, 1735 avenue Notre Dame de Vie. Age 6–12. (04 92 92 59 90)

- **Nice**: La Semeuse, rue du château. For 4–12-year-olds. (04 93 92 85 11)

- **Forum Nice-Nord**, 10 boulevard Comte de Falicon. (04 93 84 24 37)

- **Vallauris**: rue François Donnet. (04 93 64 55 24)

LES CENTRES D'INFORMATION JEUNESSE

- **Antibes**: 18/20, Boulevard Foch (04 92 90 52 38)

- **Cannes**: 5, Quai Saint Pierre (04 93 06 31 51)

- **Grasse**: 25, rue de l'Oratoire (04 93 40 13 13)

- **Nice**: 19, rue Gioffredo (04 93 80 93 93)

- **St-Raphael**: 21, Place Gallieni (04 94 19 47 38)

- **Villeneuve-Loubet**: 15, avenue de la Libération (04 92 02 05 05)

CHILDREN TRAVELLING ALONE

Major airlines will accept children travelling alone on international flights from the age of five. The child must, of course, have a passport, and a letter authorising them to leave their home country. It is wise to book the flight well in advance as the number of unaccompanied children on a flight is limited. You will need to specify the names of one or two people authorised to collect your child from the airport on arrival. SNCF operates a *Service Jeunes Voyageurs* for children from four to 14 years old. Staff take responsibility for your child from the station of departure. There is a supplement of around 40 euros to pay. For further information telephone 08 92 35 35 35 or see voyage-sncf.com.

Appendix 1
Useful addresses

BRITISH EMBASSY

35, rue Faubourg St. Honoré, 75008 Paris. (01 44 51 31 02)

British Consulate and vice-consulate

The British Embassy website at www.amb-grandebretagne.fr has useful information about living and working in France and links to the five consulates.

The Côte d'Azur falls under the auspices of the Marseille consulate: 24, av du Prado, 13006 Marseille. (04 91 15 72 10) There is a vice-consulate in Nice (04 93 82 53 06) and also a vice-consulate in Monaco at 33 bd Princesse Charlotte, BP 265 MC 98005 Monaco Cedex. (00 377 93 50 99 66 from outside Monaco.)

OTHER EMBASSIES

Australia: 4 rue Jean Rey, 75015 Paris. (01 40 59 33 00)

Canada: 35, av Montaigne, 75008 Paris. (01 44 43 29 16)

Ireland: 41, rue Rude, 75016 Paris. (01 44 17 67 00)

New Zealand: 7 ter, rue Léonard de Vinci, 75016 Paris. (01 45 00 24 11)

United States of America: 2, rue Florentin, 75001 Paris. (01 43 12 23 47)

THE FRENCH EMBASSY, UK

58 Knightsbridge, London SW1X 7JT. (0207 073 1000) The Embassy's website www.ambafrance.org.uk has some useful information.

L'INSTITUT FRANÇAIS

Queensbury Place, London SW7 2DT. (0207 834 2144; www.francealacarte.org.uk)

This has a multimedia library, newspapers, restaurant and language facilities. There are regular showings of French films and other cultural events. There are a number of French shops in the area, a children's library (0207 838 2144) and the French Bookshop (0207 584 2840).

CENTRE FRANÇAIS DE LONDRES

61 Chepstow Place, London W2 4TR. (020 7792 0337). You will also find French cultural centres in Bath, Bristol, Cambridge, Exeter, Glasgow, Jersey, Milton Keynes, Manchester, Oxford and York.

GENERAL INFORMATION

The British Council website at www.britcoun.org/france.

The Association France–Grande-Bretagne has a considerable number of branches. Contact details: 183 Daumesnil, 75012 Paris. (01 55 78 71 71)

The British Community Committee (BCC) publishes a directory of British or Franco-British associations in France which is available at the British Consulate in Paris.

Adapt in France is a voluntary advice organisation primarily for foreigners in the Alpes-Maritimes. Numerous workshops. (www.adaptinfrance.org.uk; 04 93 65 33 79)

Accueil des Villes Françaises (01 47 70 45 85). A voluntary organisation created to welcome those new to an area. Most of its members are French, though it also welcomes foreigners and organises low cost French lessons. There are branches in most main towns and cities. See the website at www.avt-accueil.com which is in French and English.

BANKS

See Chapter 10.

BUSINESS

The Franco-British Chamber of Commerce & Industry, 31 rue Boissy d'Angla, 75008 Paris. (www.francobritishchambers.com; 01 53 30 81 30)

www.entreprendre-enfrance.fr: an organisation to assist in obtaining business finance and subsidies.

CHURCHES

See Chapter 10 and also www.anglicansonline.org.uk.

EMPLOYMENT

See Chapters 3 and 4.

ENGLISH BOOKSHOPS

See Chapter 10.

ENGLISH LANGUAGE NEWSPAPERS

The News, Brussac, 3 chemin La Monzie 24000 Perigueux. (05 53 06 84 48)

The Riviera Reporter, 56 chemin de Provence, 06250 Mougins. (www.riviera-reporter.com; 04 93 45 77 19)

The Riviera Times (www.rivieratimes.com; 04 93 27 60 00)

EXPAT WEBSITES

See a good number of websites with links from the Back in Blighty website www.backinblighty.com (see 'expat links').

FINANCIAL ADVISERS

Mortgages Overseas (01279 715597)

Tee Financial (www.teefrance.co.uk; 01279 755200)

Crédit Agricole Britline (www.britline.com; 00 33 2 31 55 67 89 from the UK)

Siddals International FR (Investment@johnsiddals.co.uk; 05 56 34 75 51)

FRENCH GOVERNMENT WEBSITES

Direction Générale des Impôts: www.impots.gouv.fr

Douanes et droit indirects: www.douane.minefi.gouv.fr (Customs and indirect taxes: version in English)

DG CCRF: www.dgccrf.minefi.gouv.fr

Trésor Public: www.impots.gouv.fr

Institut National de la Statistique et des Etude Economiques: www.insee.fr

Commerce Artisanat: www.pme-commerce-artisanat.gouv.fr

Commerce Exterieur: www.dree.org

DRIRE: www.drire.gouv.fr

LEARNING FRENCH

www.europa-pages.co.uk/france has a directory of schools, colleges and universities offering French language tuition in France.

www.pcoplcgoingglobal.com/curopc/francc.htm also has a directory of universities and other establishments where one can study French in France, and access a Newcomers Club Directory for France.

Alliance Française (courses at numerous locations in France) (01 45 44 38 28)

LAWYERS

Tee France: (www.teefrance.co.uk; 01279 755200)

Fabian Cordiez: (Cordiez@mailfrance.com; 0207 748 3031)

Fauchon & Levy: (f-l@dircon.co.uk; 0207 430 0533)

Sean O'Connor: (Seanoconnor@aol.com; 01732 365378)

REMOVAL FIRMS

Allied Pickfords: (04 92 02 86 06)

Allied Arthur Pierre: (www.alliedarthurpierre.com; 0208 219 8000)

Britannia Bradshaw International: (www.bradshawinternational.com; 0161 877 5555)

Compagnie Générale: (www.grospiron.com; 04 93 72 43 43)

Overs International: (01252 343646; 04 92 08 07 81)

Worldwide Shipping & Airfreight Co: (www.worldfreight.co.uk; 0238 063 3660)

SATELLITE INSTALLERS

www.skydigitalfrance.co.uk

www.digiboxfr.com

www.susat@co.uk: (0845 451 3133)

European Satellite Installations: (02 96 86 65 93); (01242 517629)

TRANSPORT

Airlines

Air France: (www.airfrance.co.uk; 0845 084 5111)

Britair: (www.britair.fr; 08 20 82 08 20)

British Airways: (www.britishairways.com; 0845 773 3377)

British European: (www.flybe.com; 0870 567 6676)

BMI Baby: (www.flybmi.com; 0870 607 0555)

easyJet: (www.easyjet.co.uk; 0870 600 0000)

Jet 2: (www.jet2.co.uk)

Ryanair: (www.ryanair.com; 0870 156 9569)

Airports

A comprehensive list of the 143 French airports with links to each of them is accessible via: www.aeroports.fr.

Ferries

Brittany Ferries: (www.brittany-ferries.com; 0870 556 1600)

Condor: (www.condorferries.co.uk; 0845 345 2000)

Irish Ferries: (www.irishferries.com; 0870 517 1717)

Norfolkline: (www.norfolkline.com; 0870 870 1020)

P & O Ferries: (www.posl.com; 0870 600 0600)

P & O Portsmouth: (www.poportsmouth.com; 0870 242 4999)

Sea France: (www.seafrance.com; 0870 571 1711)

Transmanche: (www.transmancheferries.com; 0800 917 1201)

Ferries to Corsica

Corsica Ferries: (www.corsica-ferries.co.uk; 00 33 4 95 32 95 95)

SNCM: (www.sncm.fr; 0891 70 28 02)

Rail

www.raileurope.co.uk: (0870 584 8848)

www.frenchmotorail.com: (0870 241 5415)

www.eurotunnel.com: (0870 535 3535)

Road and Route Planning

www.theaa.com

www.rac.co.uk

www.michelin-travel.com

www.mappy.com

YELLOW PAGES

http://wfbpagesjaunes.fr

LOCAL INFORMATION

Nice

Gare SNCF: (08 92 35 35 35)

Conseil Générale des Alpes-Maritimes: 10, route de Grenoble.
(04 97 18 60 00)

Préfecture de Nice: 147, route de Grenoble. (04 93 72 20 00)

La Poste Principale: 21, avenue Thiers. (04 93 82 65 00)

Objets Trouvés: 1, rue de la Terrasse. (04 97 13 44 10)

Gare routière (bus station): (04 93 85 61 81)

Bibliothèque Municipale: 1, avenue St. Jean Baptiste.
(04 97 13 48 00)

EDF/GDF (24 hours): 10, route de Grenoble. (08 10 81 90 75)

SOS Médecins: (08 10 85 01 01)

Urgences Dentaires: (04 93 80 77 77)

Urgences Pédiatres: (04 92 03 60 89)

Antibes, Juan-les-Pins

Mairie d'Antibes: Cours Massena. (04 92 90 50 00)

Police Municipale: 39, boulevard Wilson, Antibes.
(04 92 93 05 24)

SOS Médecins: (08 25 06 70 00)

La Poste (Antibes): place des Martyrs de la Resistance.
(04 92 90 61 00)

La Poste (Juan-les-Pins): 1, avenue Maréchal Joffre.
(04 92 93 75 50)

Bibliothèque Municipale: 12, place du Gal de Gaulle, Antibes.
(04 92 90 52 40)

Objets Trouvés: 2, avenue Amiral Courbet, Antibes.
(04 97 21 75 63)

Cagnes-sur-Mer

Mairie: rue de l'Hôtel de Ville. (04 93 22 19 00)

Gendarmerie: 48, avenue de Grasse. (04 93 20 62 02)

Police Municipale: 21, square Bourdet. (04 93 22 19 22)

La Poste (principale): 6, avenue de la Serre. (04 92 02 41 27)

Gare SNCF: (08 92 353535)

Bibliothèque Municipale: avenue du Dr. Donnat. (04 92 02 37 10)

Cinéma Espace Centre: 5, avenue de Verdun. (08 92 68 01 26)

Piscine Municipale: avenue Marcel Pagnol. (04 93 73 28 28)

Cannes

Aeroport Cannes-Mandelieu: (08 20 42 66 66)

Mairie: rue Felix Faure: (04 97 06 40 00)

Commissariat de Police: 1, avenue de Grasse. (04 93 06 22 22)

Centre Hospitalier de Cannes: 13, avenue de Broussailles.
(04 93 69 70 00)

La Poste (Principale): 22, rue Bivouac Napoleon.
(04 93 06 26 50)

Gare SNCF: rue Jean Jaures. (08 92 35 35 35)

Gare Routiere (Bus station): (04 93 45 20 08)

Office du Tourisme: La Croisette. (04 93 39 24 53)

Objets Trouvés: 1, av St. Louis. (04 97 06 40 00)

Grasse

Mairie: place du Petit Puy. (04 97 05 50 00)

Police Municipale: (04 93 40 17 17)

SOS Médecins: (04 93 40 03 00)

Hôpital: (04 93 09 55 55)

Bibliotheque: boulevard Antoine Maure. (04 93 40 56 40)

Gare SNCF: 4, place de la Buanderie. (04 93 36 28 79)

Mouans-Sartoux

Mairie: (04 92 92 47 00)

Gendarmerie: (04 93 75 27 46)

Police Municipale: (04 92 92 47 27)

Office du Tourisme: (04 93 75 75 16)

Mougins

Mairie: (04 92 92 50 00)

Police Municipale: (04 92 92 57 22)

La Poste: (04 92 92 57 74)

Office du Tourisme: (04 93 75 87 67)

Villeneuve-Loubet

Mairie: (04 92 02 60 00)

Police Municipale: (04 92 02 60 60)

La Poste: (04 93 22 64 04)

Office du Tourisme: (04 92 02 66 16)

LES CAISSES D'ALLOCATIONS FAMILIALES

All one telephone number: (08 21 01 99 06)

Antibes: 660, allee des Terriers 06600

Cannes: 13, rue Butura 06400

Nice: 47, avenue de la Marne 06000

Appendix 2
Transport to and on
the Côte d'Azur

NICE CÔTE D'AZUR AIRPORT

(www.nice.aeroport.fr; 0820 42 33 33 or 00 33 4 89 88 98 28 from outside France).

Nice airport, now with a second terminal, is France's second largest airport, with many direct flights both to destinations in the UK and elsewhere in Europe. Indeed, there are currently 98 different destinations with over 50 regular airlines.

Club Airport Premier

If you are a regular visitor to Nice Airport it is worthwhile considering joining the *Club Airport Premier*. Membership is free for those who have flown from Nice airport on at least ten occasions in a year.

Advantages include:

* receiving information concerning your flight direct to your mobile telephone;

- reserved parking spaces in P2 (Terminal 1) and P5 (Terminal 2) near to the terminal entrances;

- the right to use the reserved channel at security control thereby avoiding lengthy queues;

- reduced rates of entry to the exclusive airport lounge and to the airport's business facilities;

- reductions at some of the airport's shops and restaurants.

Destinations from Nice airport

You can fly from Nice airport direct to all of London's four airports. BMI fly to Heathrow, British Airways to Heathrow and Gatwick, and easyJet to Gatwick, Luton and Stansted. The bmibaby flights are competitive but are generally not at the most convenient times. The earliest flight to London at the time of writing is the 08.00 British Airways flight scheduled to arrive at Heathrow at 09.10. The latest flight is the British Airways 20.30 flight from Heathrow, scheduled to arrive in Nice at 23.25. My personal experience of this flight has been that it rarely arrives on time, and over half my flights were more than an hour late.

Other locations in the UK and Ireland with direct flights include:

- Belfast: easyJet, www.easyjet.com;

- Bristol: easyJet, www.easyjet.com;

- Dublin: Aer Lingus, www.aerlingus.com;

- Edinburgh: Globespan, www.globespan.com;

- Glasgow: Globespan, www.globespan.com;

- Leeds/Bradford: Jet2, www.jet2.co.uk;

- Liverpool: easyJet, www.easyjet.com;

- Manchester: Jet2, www.jet2.co.uk;

- Newcastle: easyJet, www.easyjet.com;

- Nottingham: BMI, www.flybmi.com.

Aer Lingus, British Airways, BMI, Globespan, and Jet 2 fly into Terminal 1, and easyJet into Terminal 2.

Local telephone numbers are:
- Aer Lingus: (01 70 20 00 72);

- bmibaby: (08 90 71 00 81);

- BA: (04 72 68 24 08);

- BMI: (01 41 91 87 04);

- easyJet: (08 25 08 25 08);

- Jet 2: (08 25 82 60 22).

There are many flights per day to Paris, including 25 daily flights with Air France. European destinations with direct flights into Nice include Amsterdam, Barcelona, Berlin, Brussels, Copenhagen, Geneva, Lisbon, Madrid, Milan, Moscow, Munich, Naples, Rome, Stockholm and Vienna. International destinations include Casablanca, Marrakech, and New York (JFK).

Facilities at the airport

The airport has a number of shops and restaurants at each terminal, as well as exclusive lounges and business facilities. There is a pharmacy in Terminal 2 open every day of the week from 08.00–20.00, and a post office in Terminal 1.

Parking at the airport

There is ample parking at both terminals. There is also a free shuttle connecting both terminals and some of the car parks. You can park without charge in Parking P3 for 30 minutes, and in Parking P5 for 20 minutes.

An alternative to Nice Airport car parks is www.easy-parking.com. You need to book the service by internet or by telephone (04 93 26 21 98), at least 24 hours in advance. Whilst you are away you can have your car cleaned inside and out and repairs carried out.

Public transport links to Nice airport

Trains

Public transport links to the airport are not particularly good. There is no train link, though Nice St. Augustin is only a ten-minute walk from Terminal 1. From Nice St. Augustin station you can catch trains to stations along the coast to the Italian border to the east and Marseille to the west. Stops include Menton, Monaco, Eze, Beaulieu-sur-Mer, Villefranche-sur-Mer, Cagnes-sur-Mer, Villeneuve-Loubet, Biot, Antibes, Juan-les-Pins, Cannes and Mandelieu. There is also a direct service to Grasse which stops at Mouans-Sartoux. One word of caution, although the station at Nice St. Augustin is only a short walk away, it is in a rough district and should be avoided if you are travelling alone, especially at night. A safer option is to take a taxi or bus to or from the main train station in Nice.

Buses

There are bus services to the centre of Nice, to Cannes, Sophia Antipolis, Antibes, Monaco, Menton and other destinations along the coast. There is also a bus service to Marseille calling at stops along the A8 motorway, including at the Mandelieu intersection and at Le Cannet.

You can access all train and bus timetables via the airport's website www.aeroportdenice.fr.

Taxis

Taxi fares from Nice airport are expensive, in the region of 100 euros for the journey to Cannes (apparently a taxi licence costs around 200,000 euros to acquire). If you are travelling alone, a helicopter ride is sometimes no more expensive! The taxis are well maintained and comfortable, but Nice taxi drivers have a terrible reputation. A common ruse that certainly used to be frequently employed, and probably still is, is to charge the night tariff for day fares (the letter D on the meter will tell you if the driver has done this). A taxi is obliged to take you to any destination within 40 km and can only refuse those who are drunk, are accompanied by an animal, or have a very large amount of baggage. For fares over 16 euros the driver must provide a written receipt.

One alternative to taxis is Airport Transfer Services, which at the time of writing had a charge of 61 euros from Nice Airport to Cannes (www.a-t-s.net).

TOULON AIRPORT

(www.Toulon-hyeres.airport.fr; 0825 01 83 87)

Those living in the Var, or at the western side of the Alpes-Maritimes may find it convenient to use Toulon Airport from which easyJet now has direct flights to London Gatwick. Air France has seven flights a day to Paris Orly. Virgin Airlines and Jet Only (www.jetairfly.com) both have flights to Brussels. There is also a Transavia service to Rotterdam (www.transavia.com).

Parking

If you need to park your car at Toulon airport for any length of time consider the Travel Park voucher scheme. For a fixed fee of 20 euros you can park in the P2 car park opposite the terminal building for up to 16 days.

CANNES-MANDELIEU AIRPORT

(www.cannes.aeroport.fr; 0802 42 66 66)

This small airport is unsuitable for larger aircraft owing to the proximity of the nearby hills. Indeed some pilots seem to have difficulty landing here, with at least one narrowly missing the writer's car as it drove along the feeder road to the nearby A8 junction! There are regular services to relatively few destinations, but including Nice, St. Tropez and Les Îles de Lérins.

The airport is used by private aircraft. It is only a short drive (5 minutes if you are lucky) from La Croisette.

GENOA AND TURIN AIRPORTS

If you live towards the Italian border you may find it convenient to use the Ryanair service from Genoa to London Stansted. Another less attractive alternative is Turin from where Ryanair also fly to London Stansted. It is quite a long journey to Turin, and very cold in winter with the possibility of the motorway being treacherous. If you leave your car in the car park at Turin airport, do not leave valuables in it, and keep your fingers crossed that it is still there and in a driveable condition when you return.

FLIGHTS FROM NICE CÔTE D'AZUR AIRPORT TO LOCAL AIRPORTS

Hélisecurité has eight scheduled flights a day from Nice airport to Monaco and back, and nine flights a day to Cannes Palm Beach. These journeys cost 75 euros plus airport taxes each way, 140 euros return. If you are travelling alone this works out at about the same price as a taxi. Flight times are six minutes. (www.helicopter-saint-tropez.com; 00 33 4 94 55 59 99)

Azur HéliCoptère will fly you from Nice airport to St. Tropez, Marseilles or Hyeres, and from Cannes to Nice or to St. Tropez. Prices are cheapest per head if you are travelling in a group of five – for example Cannes airport to Nice would then cost 110 euros each. Nice to St. Tropez, with five people travelling works out at about 200 euros each. The company can also fly you from Nice airport to mountain ski resorts, or from Cannes to the Ile de Lérins, or to Monaco (respectively 54 and 128 euros a head in each case with three travelling). (www.azurhelico.com; 00 33 4 93 90 40 70)

BUSES ON THE CÔTE D'AZUR – A NEW DEAL!

A considerable number of bus routes are now included in the TAM network that covers 23 communes in the Alpes-Maritimes including Beaulieu-sur-Mer, Cagnes-sur-Mer, Nice, St. Laurent-du-Var, Nice, Vence and Villefranche-sur-mer. There is a standard fare of 1.30 euros irrespective of the distance travelled. This has, for example, drastically reduced the fare from Nice Airport to Cannes via the RN7 which was over 9 euros. This reduced tariff does not apply to the more direct Nice-Cannes link via the A8 Autoroute. For further information about the TAM network see the website www.cg.06.fr and also www.lignedazur.com.

FAMILY DISCOUNTS ON PUBLIC TRANSPORT

For families with three or more children substantial discounts are available for public transport with a *carte famille nombreuse*.

FERRY SERVICES

Société Nationale Maritime Corse Méditerranée (www.sncm.fr; 08 25 88 80 88) provide ferries to Corsica, Sardinia, Algeria and Tunisia. A service is also run by Corsica Ferries (04 92 00 42 93).

Compagnie Horizon IV operates services from Cannes to les Îles de Lérins (Ile Sainte Marguerite and Ile Saint Honorat) from Quai des Îles, Cannes (04 92 98 71 36). Compagnie Maritime Cannoise also has a service for Les Îles de Lérins (www.lesilesdelerins.com; 04 93 38 66 33).

For trips from Nice and Cannes to Saint Tropez, Monaco and Les Îles de Lérins contact Trans-Côte-Azur. (www.trans-cote-azur.com; 04 92 00 42 30).

Transport Maritimes Théouliens operates ferries from Théoule-sur-Mer to Les Îles de Lérins. (04 93 90 65 19)

BUS AND COACH COMPANIES' CONTACT DETAILS

Rapides Côte d'Azur: (04 93 85 64 44)

Buz Azur: (08 25 82 55 99)

Autocars S.A.P. (for regular services between Vence, St. Paul, La Colle, Cagnes-sur-Mer, Saint Laurent-du-Var and Nice): (04 93 58 37 60)

TRANSPORT FOR THE HANDICAPPED

For information on transport for handicapped people, details of the European Parking Card (*La Carte Européene de Stationnement*) and details for obtaining financial assistance for handicapped schoolchildren can be obtained from CDES (Commission Departementale d'Education Speciale) in Nice (04 92 29 43 40).

CONTACTING THOSE AT SEA

Should you need to contact anyone at sea you should consult the Service des Renseignments Radio Maritimes (08 10 01 10 21).

L'AUTOMOBILE CLUB NICE CÔTE D'AZUR

It is well worth considering membership of this club, or some similar organisation. There are various rates from around 40 euros per annum. Benefits include:

- car insurance, breakdown assistance;

- special rates at certain outlets;

- *Le Guide Practique de L'Automobliste*;

- free representation if you are charged with a driving offence, or are faced with the threat of losing your licence;

- advice should you lose important documents;

- advice on the most appropriate itinerary for your travel plans;

- road travel information.

For further information contact the club at Zone d'Action, Alpes-Maritimes, 9, rue Massenet, 06000 Nice, (www.AutomobileClubNice.com; 04 93 87 18 17). There are separate clubs for Cannes (04 93 94 14 63) and Menton (04 93 35 77 39).

Appendix 3
Clothes sizes

WOMEN

Coats, dresses, skirts

UK	8	10	12	14	16	18	20	22
US	6	8	10	12	14	16	18	20
France	34	36	38	40	42	44	46	48

Blouses and jumpers

UK(inches)	31	32	34	36	38	40	42
US(size)	6	8	10	12	14	16	18
France(cm)	81	84	87	90	93	96	99

Shoes

UK	3.5	4/4.5	5	5.5	6	6.5	7
US	5	5.5/6	6.5	7	7.5	8	8.5
France	36	37	38	39	39	40	41

MEN

Suits

UK/US	36	38	40	42	44	46	48
France	46	48	50	52	54	56	58

Shirts

UK/US	14	14.5	15	15.5	16	16.5	17	17.5
France	36	37	38	39	41	42	43	44

Shoes

UK	6	7	8	9	10	11	12
US	7	8	9	10	11	12	13
France	39	41	42	43	44	45	46

CHILDREN

Clothes

UK	16/18	20/22	24/26	28/30	32/34	36/38
US	2	4	6	8	10	12
France	92	104	116	128	140	152

Shoes

UK	2	3	4	4.5	5	6	7	7.5	8	9
US	2	3	4	4.5	5	6	7	7.5	8	9
France	18	19	20	21	22	23	24	25	26	27

UK	10	11	11.5	12	13	1	2	2.5	3	4
US	10	11	11.5	12	13	1	2	2.5	3	4
France	28	29	30	31	32	33	34	35	36	37

Appendix 4
Further reading

BOOKS ABOUT FRANCE

Biggins, Alan (2002) *Selling French Dreams,* Kirkdale Books

Brame, Genevieve (2004) *Chez vous en France*, Kogan Page

Davey, Charles (2005) *The Complete Guide to Buying Property in France,* Kogan Page

Davey, Charles (2006) *The Tee France Guide to Living and Working in France,* Stanley Tee

Hart, Alan (2004) *Going to Live in Paris* Howtobooks

Hunt, Deborah (2003) *Starting and Running a B&B in France,* Howtobooks

Mayle, Peter (2000) *A Year in Provence*, Penguin

Nadeau, Jean-Benoit & Barlow, Julie (2004) *Sixty Million French People Can't Be Wrong. What makes the French so French?* Robson Books

Platt, Polly (2003) *French or Foe?* Cultural Crossings Limited

BOOKS ABOUT THE RIVIERA

Jones, Ted (2003) *The French Riviera – A Literary Guide for Travellers*, IB Tauris & Co

McKenie, Carolyn (2004) *Portraits of the Riviera,* Penguin

Misseri, Helen and Moati, Elisabeth (2004) *Le Curieux, Monaco – French Riviera for Families*, Editions Milles et une Feuilles

Ring, Jim (2004) *Riviera: the Rise and Rise of the Côte d'Azur,* John Murray

Rick Steeves' 2007 Provence and the French Riviera, Avalon Travel Publishing (2006)

Whitehouse, Rosie (2003) *Take the Kids: South of France*, Cadogan Guide

Don't get caught out when making regular foreign currency transfers

Even once you have bought your property you need to make sure that you don't forget about foreign exchange. It's highly likely that you'll need to make regular foreign currency transfers from the UK whether for mortgage payments, maintenance expenditure or transferring pensions or salaries, and you may not realise that using your bank to arrange these transfers isn't always the best option. Low exchange rates, high fees and commission charges all eat away at your money and mean that each time you use your bank you lose out. However, by using Currencies Direct's Overseas Regular Transfer Plan you can get more of your money time after time.

Exchange Rates

Your bank is likely to only offer you a tourist rate of exchange due to the small amounts being transferred. However, Currencies Direct is able to offer you a commercial rate of exchange regardless of the amount that you wish to transfer.

Transfer Charges

Most banks will typically charge between £10 and £40 for every monthly transfer. Currencies Direct is able to offer free transfers, which will save you a considerable amount of money over time.

Commission Charges

When made through a bank transfers are usually liable for a commission charge of around 2%. By using Currencies Direct you can avoid commission charges altogether.

How does it work?

It is very easy to use Currencies Direct. The first thing you need to do is open an account with them. Once this is done all you need to do is set up a direct debit with your bank and confirm with Currencies Direct how much money you would like to send and how often (monthly or quarterly). They will then take the money from your account on a specified day and once they have received the cleared funds transfer it to France at the best possible rate available.

Information provided by Currencies Direct.
www.currenciesdirect.com   Tel: 0845 389 1729
Email: info@currenciesdirect.com

Index